# THE DISABILITY EXPERIENCE

## WORKING TOWARD BELONGING

## HANNALORA LEAVITT

### ILLUSTRATIONS BY BELLE WUTHRICH

ORCA BOOK PUBLISHERS

Published in Canada and the United States in 2021 by Orca Book Publishers.
orcabook.com

**Library and Archives Canada Cataloguing in Publication**
Title: The disability experience : working toward belonging /
Hannalora Leavitt ; illustrations by Belle Wuthrich.
Names: Leavitt, Hannalora, author. | Wuthrich, Belle, 1989- illustrator.
Series: Orca issues.
Description: Series statement: Orca issues | Includes bibliographical references and index.
Identifiers: Canadiana (print) 20200335162 | Canadiana (ebook) 2020033610X |
ISBN 9781459819283 (softcover) | ISBN 9781459819290 (PDF) | ISBN 9781459819306 (EPUB)
Subjects: LCSH: People with disabilities—Juvenile literature. | LCSH: Disabilities—Juvenile literature.
Classification: LCC HV1568 .L43 2021 | DDC j362.4—dc23

Library of Congress Control Number: 2020944960

**Summary:** This nonfiction book for teens provides a history of disability, describes types
of disabilities and examines the challenges faced by people living with disabilities.

Orca Book Publishers is committed to reducing the consumption of nonrenewable resources in the
making of our books. We make every effort to use materials that support a sustainable future.

Orca Book Publishers gratefully acknowledges the support for its publishing programs provided
by the following agencies: the Government of Canada, the Canada Council for the Arts and the
Province of British Columbia through the BC Arts Council and the Book Publishing Tax Credit.

Edited by Sarah N. Harvey
Design by Belle Wuthrich
Cover and interior illustrations by Belle Wuthrich

Printed and bound in South Korea.

24  23  22  21  •  1  2  3  4

*To Elver Greening, a pioneering mother
who refused to institutionalize her
bright, beautiful daughter, Karen,
who was born with cerebral palsy.*

# Contents

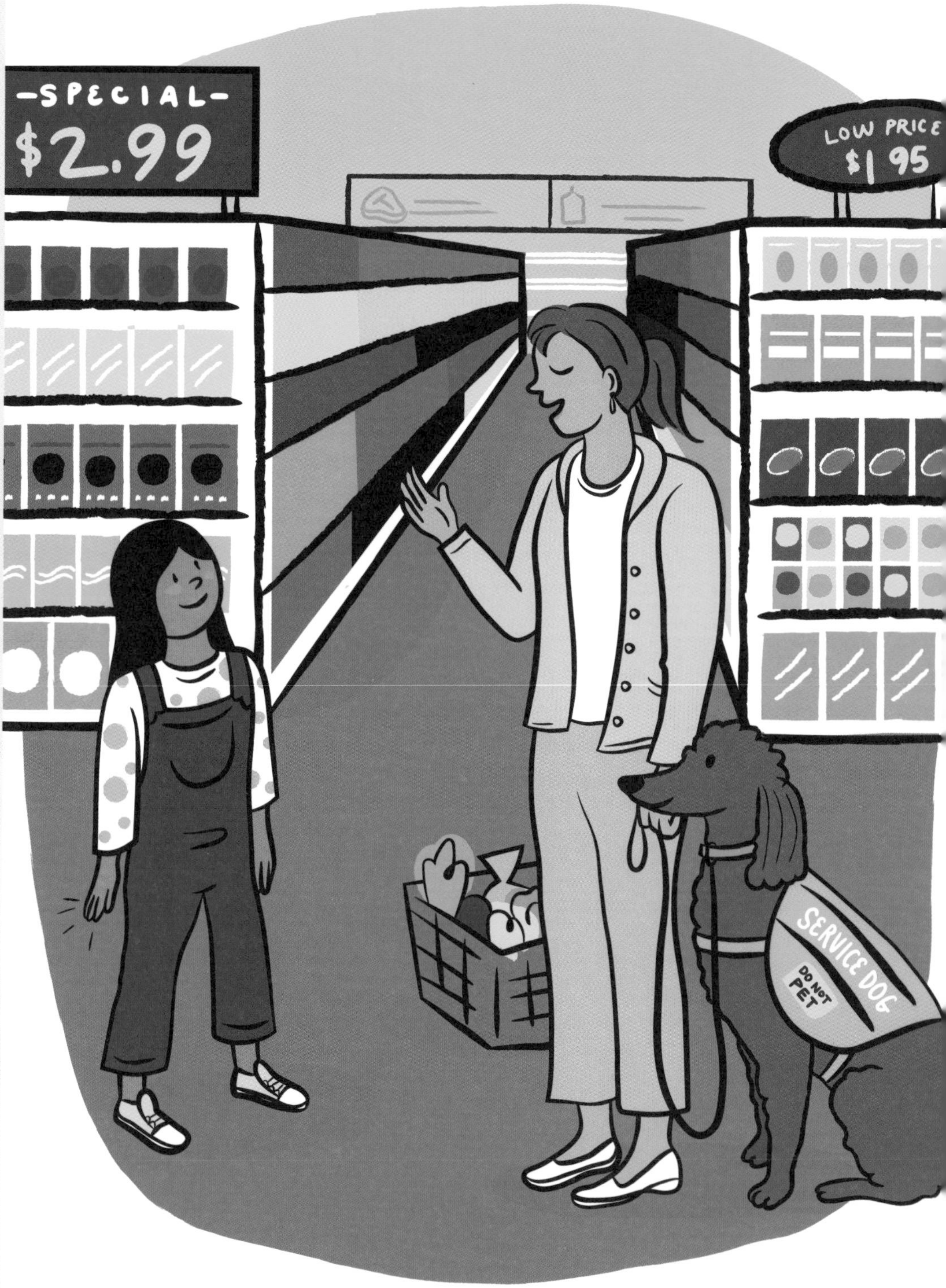
-SPECIAL-
$2.99
LOW PRICE
$1 95
SERVICE DOG
DO NOT PET

# Introduction

**A** *young girl recently* approached me at the grocery store and asked, "May I pet your guide dog?"

I thanked her for asking so politely, grateful her parents hadn't shushed her. "I'm sorry," I said. "You shouldn't pet a guide dog while it's wearing its harness. The harness means he's a working dog."

"Where does he work?" she asked.

Questions offer such great teaching moments. I'm always eager to share the real story about guide dogs because there are so many myths about them (see chapter 5 for more about guide dogs). No, my dog doesn't know how to interpret crosswalk signals. He can't read maps. He often correctly anticipates where I'm going, but this doesn't mean he can read my mind. At least, I don't think it does.

Given my eagerness to share, who better to write a book on the topic of **disability** but a writer with a visual impairment, a veteran of a disability lifestyle for nearly five decades now? I've been fortunate to have lived, learned and loved surrounded by people with all kinds of disabilities. Both my grandmother and mother contracted the polio virus, the former as a young adult and the latter as an infant. My grandmother used a wheelchair to get around, but my mother was able to walk, though with a pronounced limp. When I was a child, it never dawned on me that they were disabled. They were just my mother and grandmother. No big deal.

So we're on the same page here, let's look at the definition of disability.

# DEFINING DISABILITY

*According to the dictionary,* a disability is

1. a physical or mental condition that limits a person's movements, senses or activities;

2. a disadvantage or deficiency, especially a physical or mental impairment that interferes with or prevents normal achievement in a particular area;

3. something that hinders or incapacitates.

Definitions aside, no dictionary can possibly define what living with a disability looks and feels like. In this book we'll explore the three major types of disability—sensory, physical and intellectual. I'll be using the acronym PWD(s), which stands for person(s) with a disability or disabilities.

As you may have already noticed from the above definitions, the language associated with disability is primarily negative. For one single word, there are a lot of negative terms in the definition—impairment, prevents, limits, disadvantage, deficiency and incapacitates cast a subtle pall on the word *disability*. My goal with this book is to propose other ways of perceiving disability, ways that include and don't exclude PWDs. So how many disabled people are we talking about?

According to a 2017 update of the Canadian Survey on Disabilities (CSD) produced by Employment and Social Development Canada, I am one of 3.8 million (or one in four) Canadians (age 15 and over) living with a disability.

The United States Census Bureau reported that 8.7 percent of Americans under 65 (approximately 29 million people) were living with a disability between 2013 and 2017. Surveys measure serious difficulties with hearing, vision, cognition (thinking), walking or climbing stairs, as well as difficulty with self-care and independent living.

## Defining Otherness

With over 33 million PWDs in North America, why do so many of us feel excluded, isolated, forgotten? This phenomenon of being *marginalized* is referred to as otherness, or being othered. I am an other.

Sociologist and author Richard Jenkins states: "Ideas of similarity and difference are central to the way in which we achieve a sense of identity and social belonging. Identities have some element of exclusivity. Just as when we formally join a club or an organization, social membership depends upon fulfilling a set of criteria. It just so happens that such criteria are socially constructed (that is, created by societies and social groups). As such 'we' cannot belong to any group unless 'they' (other people) do not belong to 'our' group. Sociologists set out to study how societies manage collective ideas about who gets to belong to 'our group' and which types of people are seen as different—the outsiders of society."

*Richard Jenkins*

Disability otherness happens whether you were born with a disability (*congenital disability*) or acquired it through disease or trauma. My disability is an *acquired disability.* My experience with otherness was gradual. It started when I was in second grade, a sick kid who was often absent from school. I spent more time in the hospital than at home and slowly began to lose touch with day-to-day family and school life.

I had surgery to remove a rare, cancerous brain tumor that was slowly crushing both of my optic nerves. Despite life-saving surgery, the damage to my optic nerves was permanent. I was totally blind in my right eye and legally blind in my left, a pronouncement that set me firmly on the path of otherness, a path very different than that of my siblings and schoolmates.

In his book *The Body Silent: The Different World of the Disabled*, Dr. Robert F. Murphy, a Columbia University anthropologist, chronicled his own descent into disability when he was diagnosed with an inoperable (terminal) spinal-cord tumor. "I don't remember ever before thinking about physical disability, except as something that happened to other, less-fortunate people. It certainly had no relevance to me. A disabled person could enter my field of vision, but my mind would fail to register him—a kind of selective blindness quite common among people of our culture," Murphy writes.

With no previous awareness of disabilities, Murphy struggled to understand what being disabled would mean for him. He soon discovered he was a citizen in the world of otherness. He learned what it's like to experience barriers to being able to move freely about in his world. As he became more and more dependent on his family and care aides, he experienced an unexpected feeling—vulnerability.

I hope that reading this book will give you what Dr. Murphy didn't have before his diagnosis: the beginnings of a fundamental understanding of the types of challenges

> *As he became more and more dependent on his family and care aides, he experienced an unexpected feeling— vulnerability.*

## WHAT IS A STEREOTYPE?

*Stereotypes* are oversimplified ideas about groups of people that are based on such things as race, ethnicity, age, gender, sexual orientation—almost any characteristic.

*Like you, we struggle to discover who we are and where we might fit in and, yes, to determine our sexual identities too.*

PWDS can expect to encounter as they become expert at mastering life with a disability.

Most PWDS have the same aspirations for their lives as you do for yours. The difference is that PWDS face far more barriers to accessing equal opportunities in education, employment, housing, transportation and health care in order to achieve their goals. In addition to these barriers, the disability experience comes with centuries-old myths and stereotypes attached.

In this book we'll look to history to seek an understanding of the origins of disability and why stereotypes continue to persist today. Do blind people really hear better? Can guide dogs interpret traffic signals? Can a woman in a wheelchair have a baby? Why do so many people speak louder when addressing blind people? You'll hear stories from people with various kinds of disabilities about the myriad challenges, adaptations and solutions required to live a full, meaningful life with a disability.

Disabled people are in cultures throughout the world. You'll find us

represented in the community and the workplace and, unfortunately, more than well represented in the poverty statistics in both Canada and the United States. Like you, we struggle to discover who we are and where we might fit in and, yes, to determine our sexual identities too. And we do this in addition to managing the social and physical barriers we face each day.

I hope the information and stories featured in this book will inspire you to look at people with disabilities in a whole new, positive way. Don't place us on a pedestal, looking up at us in awe and amazement. Don't look down on us either. Rather, let's meet in the middle ground, face-to-face and ready to answer some of those shushed questions. Thank you for taking the journey into our world of otherness.

# _1_

# Let's Talk Disabilities

## WHAT IS A DISABILITY, AND WHO GETS TO HAVE ONE?

**W**_hat is a disability?_ Well, it depends on who you ask. Most of us consider a person in a wheelchair or a blind person using a guide dog to be disabled. Disabilities we are able to see easily around us in the community are called _visible disabilities_.

But there are some we do not see, including deafness, learning disabilities and intellectual impairments. They are called _invisible disabilities_, and they are often misunderstood and/or overlooked because of their hidden nature. Whether a disability is visible or invisible, its meaning shifts depending on how you look at it.

## Why Define Disability?

Why is it so important to define what a disability is? It's because governments offer support and financial services to those deemed disabled. It's important that applicants for assistance meet the definition of disability in order to receive fair and consistent levels of financial aid and services.

If they're unable to work, people with disabilities are often eligible to receive monthly financial benefits (or a pension) from provincial, federal or state governments. Receiving a disabled designation often provides individuals with specialty ground-transportation services, parking privileges and accommodations from airlines for wheelchairs and service dogs.

## The World Health Organization (WHO) Model of Disability

WHO concerns itself with global health issues. It takes a broad view when defining disability and its inherent health-care implications because it must consider political and cultural differences.

### WHO DEFINITION OF DISABILITY

"An impairment is a problem in body function or structure; an activity limitation is a difficulty encountered by an individual in executing a task or action; while a participation restriction is a problem experienced by an individual in involvement in life situations."

## The Medical Model of Disability

Health-care professionals are concerned with the diagnosis and treatment of an individual's health concerns. This approach is called the medical model. The goal of the medical model is to restore a person to their former "normal" status, to "fix" them. The medical profession does not tend to distinguish between disability and disease or illness.

### THE MEDICAL MODEL DEFINITION OF DISABILITY

"Any restriction or lack of ability to perform an activity in a manner or within the range considered normal for a human being. The term disability reflects the consequences of impairment in terms of functional performance and activity by the person."

This definition does not consider the social implications of living with a disability. Defining disability as primarily a medical condition fails to recognize the day-to-day challenges faced by PWDs living in the community.

## The Social Model of Disability

The social model of disability says that disability is caused by the way society is organized, not by an individual's medical diagnosis.

### THE SOCIAL MODEL DEFINITION OF DISABILITY

The social model rejects the idea that the "problem" is a medical one. Instead it puts forward the view that it is the way society is run and organized that is the problem, not the individual disabled person. The social model promotes the idea that disabled individuals should have choice and control in their own lives.

*The social model promotes the idea that disabled individuals should have choice and control in their own lives.*

Here's an example to help you understand the difference between the medical and social approaches to disability.

A medical report about a patient with a physical disability will often read as follows: *This 22-year-old paraplegic man sustained injuries in a motor-vehicle accident…*

A social history prepared by a social worker on the same individual may read: *I met with this 22-year-old man, who sustained* **paraplegia** *in a motor-vehicle accident…*

Both reports are accurate, but one specialty sees the disability first, and the other recognizes the individual first. The social model of disability, often called "person first," has been adopted by the legal communities in both Canada and the United States.

So who gets to have a disability? The truth is that disability does not discriminate. We are all vulnerable.

## ORIGINS OF DISABILITY

**N**ow that you have a better understanding of the different approaches to defining disability, let's look at the many kinds of disability.

### Congenital Disabilities

Congenital disabilities, also referred to as birth defects, may be present at birth but are not always immediately recognized by medical professionals. They are caused by chromosomal defects, gene abnormalities and genetic factors interacting with the environment. A small percentage of disabilities is caused by maternal use of alcohol and drugs, maternal infections and other illnesses.

Examples of congenital disorders include albinism, cleft lip/palate, Down syndrome, cystic fibrosis and spina bifida.

## Acquired Disabilities

Acquired disabilities are ones whose onset occurs after birth. Accident-related disabilities such as head injuries and spinal-cord injuries are two examples of acquired disabilities. Another cause of this kind of disability is disease, such as meningitis, rubella and moderate to severe arthritis.

# TYPES OF DISABILITIES

**P**WDS **are as** distinct from one another as are able-bodied people, but we are often lumped together under the general term *disabled*. For instance, I am often asked if I would prefer to take the elevator instead of the stairs. My disability is vision loss. It's an impairment of the sense of sight. It does not affect the functioning of my limbs. My ability to move easily about, to navigate curbs and stairs and escalators, is not affected by my vision loss. However, if I cannot see them, I could easily trip and/or fall. Not seeing them is different from not being able to navigate them.

The confusion about my ability to navigate stairs is the equivalent of asking a person in a wheelchair if they would like a **braille** restaurant menu. This is one example of why it's so important that we understand the distinction between sensory, physical and intellectual disabilities.

When you understand that a visually impaired person has a *sensory disability*, of course you will appreciate their need to ask for assistance from time to time because they are unable to read signage and other information. A deaf and/or deafblind individual will more than likely struggle with communicating their needs to a hearing and seeing world. A person with a physical disability will appreciate the lowered

panel in an elevator but will not need to use the braille markings on it. And someone with an *intellectual disability* who has full vision may be able to see and read the schedule posted at a bus stop but may require more time and patience to process the meaning of the information.

## WHAT IS A SENSORY DISABILITY?

A *sensory disability is* a severe impairment or loss of the sense of sight and/or hearing. Some PWDS have lost a significant amount of vision. Others have lost most of their ability to hear. And a minority of others have experienced a combination of both vision and hearing loss.

## The Sense of Sight

Significant impairment of one's vision is commonly referred to as visual impairment or *legal blindness.*

I first noticed something amiss with my vision when I was 11 and struggling to read the blackboard. I could see that something was written on the board because of the contrast between the lightness of the chalk and the darkness of the board, but it was a blur. It was the same with the print in my textbooks. I could see the print because the letters were dark against a white background. But they were as blurry as the words on the blackboard.

I couldn't recognize my friends or teachers because their faces were blurs too. Teachers were taller than students—that was the only way I could tell them apart.

I thought maybe I just needed a pair of glasses, but I was wrong. A visit to the local eye specialist changed my status from sighted student to being registered as legally blind.

Optometrists assess vision in two ways: visual acuity and visual field.

*Visual acuity* refers to distance and clarity of vision. It is typically represented as a fraction. If you have perfect vision, you have a visual acuity of 20/20. Acuity is tested with the use of a Snellen chart, the poster you'll find in almost every medical office. The chart assesses

## WHAT IS LEGAL BLINDNESS?

Legal blindness is a level of blindness that has been defined by law to limit some activities (such as driving) for safety reasons or to determine eligibility for disability-related government programs and benefits.

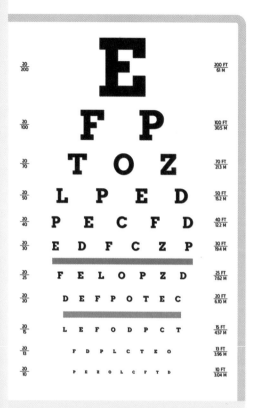

The Snellen eye examination chart was created by Herman Snellen in 1862 to measure visual acuity and is still in use today.

visual acuity by determining the level of visual detail that a person sees.

The threshold for legal blindness in North America is a visual acuity of 20/200 or less in the better eye (with the best possible correction). Having 20/200 vision means that a person has to be 20 feet away from something to be able to see it, whereas a person with full vision can see the same object from as far away as 200 feet. If you are unable to read the top letter on the Snellen chart at 20 feet, you are considered legally blind.

*Visual field* refers to the range of your vision in all directions. It is often referred to as side vision or peripheral vision. Visual fields are measured in degrees. With both eyes open, a person with normal vision can see almost 180 degrees horizontally and about 150 degrees vertically. A visual field that is constricted to the central 20 degrees or less (commonly referred to as "tunnel vision") also falls into the designation of legal blindness.

Canada's population of legally blind individuals numbers approximately 500,000, according to the Canadian National Institute for the Blind (CNIB). It's anticipated that approximately 50,000 individuals will become blind each year due to age-related eye diseases.

# AT THE TOP OF THEIR GAME

Brian McKeever

Stevie Wonder

**BRIAN MCKEEVER**—blind cross-country skier; the first-ever disabled winter athlete named to both the Paralympic and Olympic teams

**ERIK WEIHENMAYER**—the first blind person to reach the summit of Mount Everest

**JEFF HEALEY**— blind virtuoso blues-rock guitarist

**RAY CHARLES**— blind pianist and singer/songwriter

**STEVIE WONDER**— blind pop star

**CASEY HARRIS**— blind rock-star pianist in X Ambassadors

*Tunnel vision causes the loss of peripheral vision, which results in a constricted circular field of vision.*

According to the National Federation of the Blind (NFB), 1.3 million people in the United States are legally blind, and the expectation is that 75,000 will lose their vision each year, again due to age-related diseases.

So what's it like to be legally blind? In my case, I am totally blind in my right eye, but I still have minimal vision in my left. My visual acuity is significantly lower than 20/20 and is referred to as "counting fingers" vision. I'm able to count the number of fingers the eye doctor is holding up a few inches in front of my left eye. I know it doesn't sound like much to you, but it really is everything to me.

With my counting-fingers vision, I'm often startled when I'm walking down the street with my guide dog, Ogden. I'll suddenly notice a large shadowy figure that seems to have appeared out of nowhere. I can see there are people on the sidewalk immediately around us, but they are only fuzzy shapes to me. I cannot see their faces, and their clothing is usually just a slightly more colorful blur.

Most of us who are legally blind have challenges with reading the addresses on buildings, store signage, and street and bus-stop signs. Other challenges include reading package instructions, best-before dates on food, labels on prescription bottles, and newspapers, flyers and mail. And—you guessed it—we cannot drive. Well, not yet anyway. I'm anxiously awaiting the launch of the self-driving car. I can imagine my first fender bender. "But, officer, I didn't see that car coming."

## The Sense of Hearing

The second type of sensory disability is hearing impairment, or *legal deafness*. Deafness, too, has its unique challenges. Like vision impairment, the degree of hearing loss can range from partial to total deafness.

## AT THE TOP OF THEIR GAME

**MARLEE MATLIN** — award-winning deaf actor

**HEATHER WHITESTONE** —first deaf Miss America (1995)

**NYLE DIMARCO** —deaf model, actor and activist; winner of *America's Next Top Model* and *Dancing with the Stars*

**MILLIE BOBBY BROWN** —partially deaf star of *Stranger Things*

Millie Bobby Brown

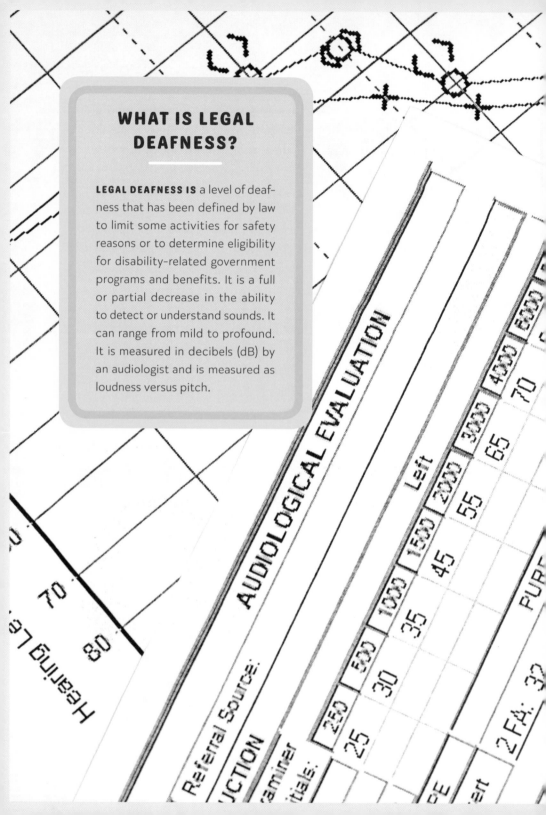

## WHAT IS LEGAL DEAFNESS?

**LEGAL DEAFNESS IS** a level of deafness that has been defined by law to limit some activities for safety reasons or to determine eligibility for disability-related government programs and benefits. It is a full or partial decrease in the ability to detect or understand sounds. It can range from mild to profound. It is measured in decibels (dB) by an audiologist and is measured as loudness versus pitch.

According to the Canadian Hearing Society, there are approximately 350,000 deaf Canadians. The 2018 Annual Disability Statistics Compendium reports that in 2017 there were 11.5 million deaf people in the United States.

## What Is Deafblindness?

A person who is deafblind has a substantial degree of loss in both vision and hearing, which results in significant difficulties in communicating, socializing, navigating and accessing information. However, few deafblind individuals are totally deaf and totally blind.

It is more problematic to develop a measurement scale for *deafblindness* than for blindness or deafness because the variables in vision-and-hearing loss are simply too numerous and complex.

The National Association of Regulatory Utility Commissions estimates that 70,000 to 100,000 people living in the United States are deafblind.

## AT THE TOP OF THEIR GAME

*Haben Girma*

← **HABEN GIRMA**—first deafblind person to graduate from Harvard Law School (2013)

**PIER MORTEN**—first deafblind person to earn a black belt in judo; five-medal Paralympian with 20 years of international competition

**HELEN KELLER**—author, writer and activist; first deafblind person in North America to attain a university degree

**MAE BROWN**—first Canadian and second deafblind woman in North America to attain a university degree

The Canadian Centre on Disability Studies estimates that 1 in every 3,000 Canadians is deafblind. Because not all deafblind people self-identify as deafblind, it's difficult to find accurate statistics for North America. This is a figure expected to increase as the Canadian population ages.

# WHAT IS AN INTELLECTUAL DISABILITY?

*ntellectual disabilities are* limitations in *cognitive ability, or intellectual functioning,* and *adaptive behavior.* They affect more males than females and have been diagnosed in between 1 and 3 percent of the population. The National Down Syndrome Society states that approximately 6.5 million Americans have some type of intellectual disability. The 2012 Canadian Survey on Disabilities reported that 160,500 persons (or 0.6 percent of Canadian adults) identified as intellectually disabled. Intellectual functioning refers to a person's ability to plan, comprehend and reason. Adaptive behavior refers to an individual's ability to apply social and practical skills in everyday life.

## LEVELS OF INTELLECTUAL DISABILITY

**MILD COGNITIVE DISABILITY:**
IQ scores between 55 and 70

**MODERATE COGNITIVE DISABILITY:**
IQ scores between 30 and 55

**SEVERE COGNITIVE DISABILITY:**
IQ scores less than 30

The IQ test is used to determine someone's level of functioning and capacity for adaptive behavior. Generally, a child with scores of 70 to 75 or lower is classified as having a cognitive disability.

## Types of Cognitive Disabilities

Approximately 15 to 20 percent of the population has some form of language-based disability. **Dyslexia** is the most common form. It is primarily a reading disability, and evidence suggests that it is an inherited condition.

**Attention deficit hyperactivity disorder** (ADHD) affects a person's ability to focus, sit still and pay attention. They may have trouble organizing activities or tasks and may interrupt other people. They may fidget, feel restless or talk excessively.

**Brain injury** is caused by such things as stroke, illness, blows or jolts to the head, brain tumors and meningitis. Each brain injury is unique—there is no reliable way to predict how an individual's brain will be affected by a particular injury.

Psychological and neurological testing determines the areas of the brain that have been damaged by an injury. The extent of the brain injury determines the outcome of the person's ability to process information.

**Genetically acquired disabilities** such as Down syndrome and autism affect people individually. Some people with these disabilities are able to function at higher levels than others. People with Down syndrome, for example, may function at a level high enough to live independently, while others with the syndrome need consistent supports to manage the *activities of daily living (ADL)*. The greater the severity of the cognitive disability, the more difficult it is for the individual to function.

# AT THE TOP OF THEIR GAME

*Whoopi Goldberg*

**DR. TEMPLE GRANDIN**—autism advocate, animal rights activist, author (autism)

**DR. STEPHEN HAWKING**—theoretical physicist, cosmologist, author (ALS)

← **WHOOPI GOLDBERG**—actor and activist (dyslexia)

**ROBIN WILLIAMS**—actor and comedian (ADHD)

**TOM CRUISE**—actor (severe dyslexia)

**JOHN FLUEVOG**—shoe designer (severe dyslexia)

## WHAT IS A PHYSICAL DISABILITY?

**A** *physical disability is* a significant limitation in a person's physical functioning. It often affects **mobility**, dexterity and/or stamina by permanently preventing normal body movement and/or control. Physical disabilities can be congenital or acquired.

### Types of Physical Disabilities

There are too many causes of physical disabilities to list in this book. Some of the more common are muscular dystrophy, spinal-cord injuries, multiple sclerosis, spina bifida and cerebral palsy.

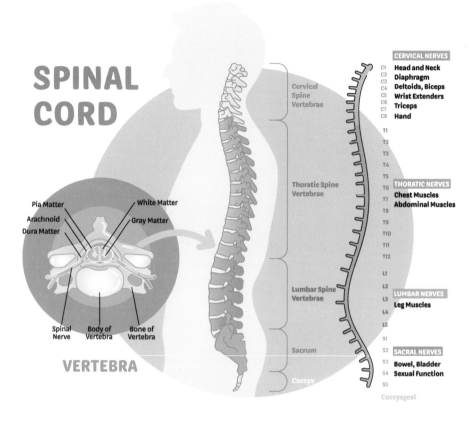

SPINAL CORD

**CERVICAL NERVES**

C1 Head and Neck
C2
C3 Diaphragm
C4 Deltoids, Biceps
C5 Wrist Extenders
C6
C7 Triceps
C8 Hand

Cervical Spine Vertebrae

Pia Matter
Arachnoid
Dura Matter
White Matter
Gray Matter

Spinal Nerve
Body of Vertebra
Bone of Vertebra

VERTEBRA

**THORATIC NERVES**

Chest Muscles
Abdominal Muscles

Thoratic Spine Vertebrae

Lumbar Spine Vertebrae

**LUMBAR NERVES**

Leg Muscles

Sacrum

**SACRAL NERVES**

Bowel, Bladder
Sexual Function

Coccyx

Coccyxgeal

In the case of spinal-cord injuries, the severity of the disability is relative to the location of the injury. Each injury is unique, but this diagram provides an idea of what types of function are lost when an injury is sustained at certain points along the spinal cord. The spine's principal function is to protect the spinal cord. But it can only do its job in normal, everyday situations.

In some cases, and with disabilities due to multiple sclerosis and other conditions, it's not the location of the injury that determines whether an individual is deemed physically disabled, but rather the individual's ability to independently perform the activities of

**IN REAL LIFE**

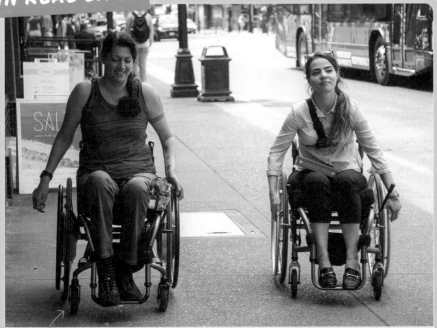

**W**ENDY COX injured her spinal cord in her early 20s when she fell from a third-story apartment balcony. Her spine was unable to protect the spinal cord, and she sustained a broken neck (damage to her cervical spine). After surgery and three months of rehabilitation, Wendy returned home. She required assistance to dress and eat and perform most other activities of daily living. She continued to work hard over the next year to develop more upper-body strength and adapt to life in a wheelchair. The damage to Wendy's spinal cord is permanent, but she has regained more upper-body movement and dexterity than was initially anticipated considering the level of spinal-cord injury. She uses a power-assist wheelchair to ease the physical demands of movement on her body.

daily living. The key activities assessed are eating, bathing, dressing, using the toilet, transfer ability (moving from bed to bathroom, for example) and maintaining control of both bladder and bowels.

A neurologist typically determines whether someone's injury meets the definition of physical disability. This decision is rendered following surgery (if applicable), multiple examinations, testing and extensive physical rehabilitation.

## IN REAL LIFE

**E**RNIE DOCTOR was diagnosed with multiple sclerosis (MS) in his mid-20s while in the Royal Canadian Air Force. An air-force physician noticed irregularities in Ernie's optic nerves, and further testing resulted in a diagnosis of MS, which is an incurable disease that can affect the brain, spinal cord and optic nerves.

In Ernie's case, progressive damage to his optic nerves resulted in a further diagnosis of legal blindness. He also experienced progressive worsening of balance and muscle control during the following decades. Now in his early 70s, Ernie experiences chronic back pain and can no longer walk safely for any distance. He uses a wheelchair in his condo but is still able to perform all activities of daily living. In Ernie's case, he is disabled because of the severity of his visual impairment, not his physical functioning.

We live in a time of unprecedented societal and technological change, and these changes hold great hope and promise for PWDS. We'll learn more about them in a later chapter. First, let's take a trip into the past and learn more about the history of disability.

# AT THE TOP OF THEIR GAME

Adrian Anantawan

**RICK HANSEN**— completed the 40,000-kilometer Man in Motion World Tour in his wheelchair in 1987; founder of the Rick Hansen Foundation and co-founder of National Access Awareness Week

**CHRISTOPHER REEVE**— actor best known for his role as Superman; became quadriplegic after a riding accident

**DAVID SHANNON**— the first quadriplegic in history to reach the geographic North Pole, where he planted a Wheelchair Parking sign

**ADRIAN ANANTAWAN**— award-winning violinist, born without his right hand, who has won numerous scholarships and is considered one of the finest violin soloists of his generation

**TANNI GREY-THOMPSON**— born with spina bifida; won 16 medals as a wheelchair racer in the Paralympic Games and is now a well-known activist and politician in the UK

# —2—

# A Brief History of Disability

**have read a lot** of books and articles in order to learn more about living with a disability in our modern, technology-savvy world. All that reading made me wonder how people with disabilities (PWDs) lived in times past. Did they live independently or with their families? Were they accepted or shunned by society? Were they able to go to school, work, have a family? I quickly realized I could write a book on this topic alone and have chosen to keep the history of disability brief in order to focus on contemporary disability.

In order to find answers to my many questions, I turned to the academic field of what is called *disability studies* (and did a lot more reading).

Researchers have long studied disabilities, but usually from a medical perspective. In the late 1980s the social model of disability became popular, and the academic discipline of disability studies was born. This discipline focuses on examining the meaning, nature and consequences of physical and intellectual disabilities from various viewpoints, such as sociology, science, political science, history and the law.

Since the beginnings of disability studies 30 years ago, researchers have made many discoveries about the lives of people with disabilities in times past. While we move through time, let's search for the possible origins of negative beliefs and stereotypes about disability and try to understand why so many persist.

Socrates

# DISABILITIES IN CLASSICAL ANTIQUITY

**T**hough human civilizations existed before Greek and Roman times, we are limited to starting there because there are no written records prior to this.

Greece and Rome are together regarded as the foundations of Western civilization. During the period known as classical antiquity (8th century BCE to the 5th century CE), their contributions to society were numerous and included the beginnings of modern philosophy (Socrates, Plato and Aristotle)

*Athletes at the ancient Olympic Games compete in front of a large crowd.*

and medicine, great leaps in mathematics, physics and astronomy, and the concept of democracy. The Olympic Games were introduced in this era, as was the practice of using coins as currency and the legal concept of innocent until proven guilty. Homer wrote *The Iliad* and *The Odyssey* during this period.

Classical antiquity was truly an era of monumental growth for humanity. But how did people with disabilities fare in those times?

Both Greek and Roman cultures placed great importance on beauty and physical perfection, which is reflected in their art. Their religious, cultural and political beliefs about disability also favored the healthy, able-bodied citizen. Just as physical fitness and health were believed to be signs of the gods' favor, disability was a mark of the gods' displeasure. For this reason, a disabled infant was often seen as a form of divine punishment for its parents. Such infants were often left outside to die.

With such negative attitudes toward the imperfect body, it's not surprising to learn that most disabled people in the Greek and Roman world existed on the margins of society, condemned to lives of poverty and exclusion. The concept of disabled people earning money by publicly displaying their different bodies (see sidebar "The Freak Show") began in this era.

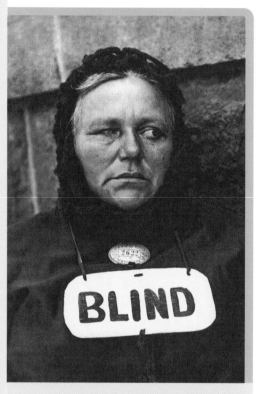

*Even in the 20th century, PWDs continued to be treated as freaks, as this 1916 photo by Paul Strand shows.*

Most disturbing, though, was the practice of using disabled people for status and entertainment purposes. Here are a few recorded examples:

- No fashionable household was complete without a few hunchbacks, dwarfs and mute people in residence.

- There was a special market in Rome for buying disabled slaves. It was commonly believed that a disabled slave acted as a good-luck charm, averting evil from its owner.

- Conopas, believed to be the shortest man alive, served as a pet to the granddaughter of Emperor Augustus.

- Disabled slaves were usually expected to earn their keep

by providing amusement and entertainment at dinner parties and other gatherings. Emperor Commodus liked to display two hunchbacks smeared in mustard on a silver platter at his banquets.

I wonder whether it was better to live in poverty on the margins of society or endure the humiliation of being used as a table centerpiece.

People with mobility impairments sometimes earned their living as potters, leather workers and metal workers because of the sedentary nature of those jobs. But they were the exception. Most disabled people would have been forced to survive through a mixture of begging, crime, casual work and family assistance.

## DISABILITY IN THE MIDDLE AGES

**W**ith the sack of Rome in 410 CE came the early days of Christianity, which had its own unique attitudes toward disabled people. The medieval era (fifth to fifteenth centuries CE) was a time of oppression, poverty and intellectual decline. It heralded only minor changes in the lives of disabled people. Disability was still a common sight in society. War injuries, disease, inbreeding, birth defects and work-related injuries persisted. Doctors and midwives often committed infanticide (baby killing) if a baby was born with a disability. Blind and deaf babies fared better because their conditions weren't detectable at birth. In this period, before vaccines, antibioics, anesthetics and prenatal care, disability was just a disease away. Anyone could be next.

This was a period when work life shifted from the home to the workplace, and workers began to receive hourly pay. This also meant that employers expected maximum productivity from workers with healthy bodies. It's reasonable to expect that workers with disabilities would not have been hired because they would not be able to achieve the same levels of productivity as their able-bodied counterparts. Researchers believe that most people with disabilities who were capable of working did so in the agricultural industry, planting and harvesting crops.

The late Middle Ages also gave us the developing concept of public services. What we now call *social housing* started in this period as society began to take responsibility for caring for and housing people with disabilities.

## THE FREAK SHOW

The Middle Ages was also the era of "the freak show," where members of the public paid for the opportunity to view various types of disabilities. If you were a member of the aristocracy, you could pay for a "freak" to come to your home for a personal viewing, often as part of a social occasion.

Historian Dr. Naomi Baker says that PWDs were "openly referred to as 'jokes of nature,' and people didn't think there was anything repugnant or sinister about them. They were simply part of the variety of the world and people wanted to enjoy and look at them."

The majority of the humans who were on display were very young children, often newborn babies with abnormalities, who were known as "monstrous births." Parents received large sums of money to display their disabled children.

# DISABILITY DURING THE RENAISSANCE

Queen Elizabeth I

**T**he Renaissance and the Age of Discovery in Europe (14th to 17th centuries) saw a significant revival of interest in the arts, architecture, philosophy, literature and the sciences. People such as Michelangelo, Isaac Newton and Leonardo da Vinci played major roles in the arts and sciences. With increased interest in the sciences, religion began to play a lesser role in everyday life. The study of medicine took hold in this era. With an increased and improved understanding of the human body, ideas about disability shifted from a flawed soul to a flawed body.

In England in the late 1500s, PWDs unable to work and the aged became the beneficiaries of Queen Elizabeth I's new Poor Laws. Government was now legally obliged to provide supports to those unable to work and make a living.

# DISABILITY DURING THE INDUSTRIAL REVOLUTION

**T**he Industrial Revolution was a period of urban industrialization that began in Great Britain from the late 1700s to mid-1800s and spread throughout the world. Large numbers of people went from

**Peter White**

living in mostly rural settings, where family members with disabilities could still be of assistance within the home, to living in cities where an unreliable farming income was traded for paid, hourly work in the factories. But as people crowded into the cities, poverty and disease followed.

Peter White is a visually impaired reporter for BBC Radio. In his podcast entitled *Disability: A New History*, White interviews numerous disability historians about what it was like to live with a disability in 18th- and 19th-century England. Disabled beggars were a common sight during the Industrial Revolution.

Tim Hitchcock is an expert on the street culture of 18th- and 19th-century London. He says, "Every beggar has to grab your attention in the first 30 seconds, that moment your eye passes their presence on the street. And disabled beggars absolutely did use their physicality in order to get what they wanted. It could be down to how you present a disabled arm or limb, it could be down to how you strapped up a blind eye or a weeping wound. The display of disabilities in public by individual beggars was one way they could earn some money to survive."

Many PWDs were placed in poorhouses, while others were "warned off"—told to leave the community.

Another phenomenon of the era was the miracle cure. People believed that disabilities could be cured by a simple touch from the queen or another luminary. The cost of accessing such an encounter was prohibitive, and many PWDs tried instead to find a rich benefactor to provide them with a living allowance.

*Deaf and mute students learn to become tailors in a school for deaf and mute youth in Paris, 1944.*

# THE DAWN OF
# EDUCATIONAL ENLIGHTENMENT

**W**ith increased interest in philosophy and the human condition, medical doctors, philosophers and educators began to believe that with education and training, physically and intellectually impaired people could achieve far more. In 1783 an institute for blind youth was established in London. Twelve young people were taken from impoverished families to study there. Other disabled youth were trained too. Skills taught included bushel basket making, knitting, sewing, bookbinding and, above all, printing. Musicianship was also encouraged.

Gutenberg's invention of the printing press in the mid-1400s made books and learning more accessible to and affordable for the general public, and most children were able to learn to read and write. Educating blind children was more difficult because they could not read print.

Prior to the development of braille (see chapter 5 for more about braille), raised or embossed print letters offered the only tactile reading experience for blind students. It was a slow and inefficient method of reading. Schools for deaf students and those with other disabilities slowly began to operate throughout Europe.

North America's first school for blind children opened in Boston, Massachusetts, in 1829 and is still in operation today. Canada's first boarding school for the blind opened its doors in Halifax, Nova Scotia, in 1871.

The first school for the deaf was established in 1817 in Hartford, Connecticut. Prior to the opening of Canada's first school for the deaf in Quebec in 1831, deaf students needed to travel to either Europe or the United States to attain an education.

The centralization and/or *segregation* of blind and deaf students in special schools meant that students left their families and hometowns and lived in residences for the duration of their education, returning home only for holidays if families could afford it. These boarding schools gave students an opportunity to meet, live and learn alongside other students with similar disabilities.

Though separated from family, they were no longer isolated, and they developed confidence and skills while they were educated with their peers, an experience not available to them in their own communities.

Those with intellectual impairments did not fare nearly as well in the realm of education. They were typically institutionalized and received no education because it was believed that they could not learn. It wasn't until the mid-to-late 1800s that influential physicians and educators proposed that learning was possible if the intellectually impaired were in the right environment.

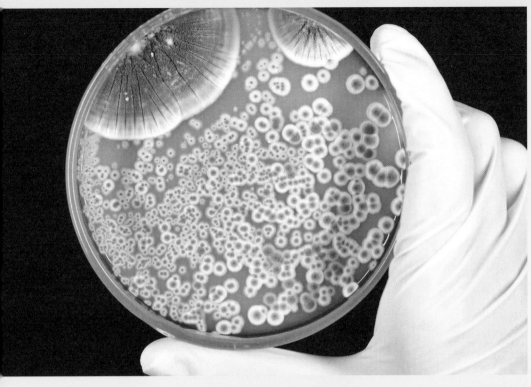

*Colonies of* Penicillium *mold grow on an agar plate in a lab.*

## WELCOME TO THE 20TH CENTURY

**B**efore 1928, doctors had no way to treat bacteria-caused illnesses, including pneumonia, brain and spinal-cord infections, rheumatic fever, blood infections and sexually transmitted diseases such as gonorrhea and syphilis. With no cure prior to antibiotics, these conditions caused innumerable disabilities. In 1928 Dr. Alexander Fleming of St. Mary's Hospital in the UK developed the first antibiotic in history—penicillin.

Dr. Alexander Fleming

43

Vaccines against devastating childhood diseases were the second great medical advance of the 20th century. In 1953 an American doctor named Jonas Salk announced that he had successfully tested a vaccine to prevent polio, a crippling disease of the nervous system. The polio virus is highly contagious and causes disability and sometimes death. Vaccines were soon available for mumps and rubella, both of which can cause disabilities.

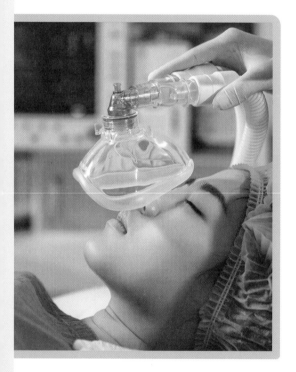

The third major medical advancement that improved the health and daily lives of persons with disabilities was the surgical anesthetic. Experimentation with various medications and inhalable gases dates back to the Greco-Roman period. It wasn't until 1842 that the first known administration of a gas for surgical pain relief was carried out by Crawford Long, who used ether during a surgery to remove a tumor from the neck of a patient.

The development of a safe surgical anesthetic made the field of orthopedic surgery possible. Broken bones could be set more accurately and easily if the patient was anesthetized. The scope of orthopedic surgery grew quickly because so many war-injured veterans and disabled people required and benefited from these corrective procedures.

The 20th century also lays claim to a number of historically significant events that saw a major increase in the number of people with disabilities. The first wave of disabled people were the victims of war injuries. The incubator debacle (see chapter 6) caused yet another generation of blind children. A rubella (German measles) epidemic doubled the number of school-age children who lost their hearing to this disease. And now, with an increased life expectancy, an entire generation is aging into disability.

While this chapter is about the historical treatment of people with disabilities, it's also the history of society's negative perceptions of the disabled body. The belief that disability is somehow a product of or punishment for sin is still prevalent today, and people with disabilities continue to be marginalized today as well.

As I did the research for this chapter, I was disappointed about the constant emphasis on the body. I am a person with a disability, but I am, first and foremost, me. The damage to my optic nerves that caused my blindness is another detail about me, like the color of my eyes and hair and my love of peanut-butter cookies. It's been my experience that once people know I have a disability, it's a challenge to get them to see me as a regular person. Since many people have a limited understanding of the daily implications of living well with a disability, I decided the best remedy for this is to share my experiences with them as much as possible.

So how do we bridge the gap between society and the person in the disabled body? Well, one way is to meet some disabled people.

In the next chapter, which examines the *culture of disability*, you'll learn more about real people with disabilities and the different ways they live their lives.

# 3

# The Culture of Disability

**W**hen the term *"culture"* is used, most people think either of a specific group of people who share a similar language, ethnicity and geography, or they think of things like music, dance and literature. There's more to culture than that though. Culture is shared. It provides a specific group with an identity, a sense of unity and belonging. Knowing I'm part of a larger group that shares similar life experiences and challenges means I'm not alone in my journey. Who wants to be alone? Not me.

## WHAT IS DISABLED CULTURE?

*The concept of disability* as its own culture started in the early 1980s, following in the footsteps of earlier civil-rights initiatives, such as racial desegregation. The concept strives to empower PWDS

(Top and below) Pictograms indicating accessibility for PWDs are becoming more inclusive and accurate.

by giving them a collective voice. It challenges society's historical practice of medicalizing and institutionalizing PWDS. PWDS share a history of social and political oppression.

Speaking with a collective voice, we have slowly changed society's practice of referring to PWDS as *crippled*, *invalid*, *impaired*, *limited* and *retarded*, replacing those words with more accurate and inclusive people-first ones. As you learned in chapter 2, the field of disability studies has emerged as part of this new identity, helping to piece together our cultural history.

In addition to the development of accurate and **inclusive** language, the pictogram (a symbol representing a word or phrase, such as the silhouette of a wheelchair) is readily accepted as indicating a service or space accessible to someone with a disability.

For the most part, disabled culture rejects the centuries-old, often patriarchal (male-dominated), approach to disability in favor of self-determination. Instead of being told where and with whom we should be living, we want to make our own choices. We're the experts when it comes to which services and supports work best for us.

PWDS want to decide where to live and work, who will provide personal-care services and whether to marry and have a family. Imagine coming from a past where such decisions were made by others, where you had no say in how your future would look. Now imagine what it's like to make your own choices. Amazing!

Before you can become a member of the disabled culture, though, you must be declared to be disabled. You learned earlier that receiving a disability label can propel someone into the margins of society and into a distinctive place with different *cultural norms* (shared expectations and rules that guide behaviors). It's also a place where relationships with family, friends and other service providers often change. In fact, a change in relationships is experienced by most, if not all, PWDS to various degrees, whether the disability is congenital or acquired.

## DISABILITY IN A MEDICAL SETTING

*hink about your doctor's* waiting room for a moment. Now try to envision someone using a wheelchair in that space. Is the doorway into the office relatively clear of obstructions? Is the reception desk taller than the person sitting in the wheelchair? How can they communicate their presence if they cannot be seen? Is the waiting room already crowded with chairs? Can someone in a wheelchair find space to wait? And let's not forget the washroom. Is it fully accessible to someone in a wheelchair, someone using a walker, someone who can't read the signs?

What about the examination room itself? There's no possible way someone in a wheelchair could fit into my doctor's exam room. It's too cramped. So what then? All that is left is for the patient to sit in the doorway during the consultation, forgoing privacy and confidentiality.

And what if the patient needs a complete physical exam and cannot mobilize sufficiently to scale the exam table? Wendy Cox's doctor recently referred her to the local women's clinic for a procedure. She was thrilled to discover it had adjustable-height exam tables, because she wasn't confident she could safely transfer from her wheelchair onto the traditional high one.

Wendy's friend is in a power wheelchair and cannot independently transfer to the exam table. Her only option is to go to her local hospital, where they use a lift to transfer her to the table.

## FULLY ACCESSIBLE HEALTH CARE

The management at one clinic has thought about how to deliver health care to people with physical disabilities. The Access Clinic at BC Women's Hospital and Health Centre is the only provider of fully accessible health care in Vancouver, British Columbia. The clinic is wheelchair-accessible, with lifts that allow women to transfer to accessible beds, and stirrups that accommodate patients with spasticity due to cerebral palsy or other conditions. The center provides gynecological care to adolescents and women with disabilities. Staff also treat transgender patients and those who've experienced sexual trauma. Creating physical access to health-care services is only one aspect of access.

## IN REAL LIFE

**D**ISABILITYAFTERDARK PODCASTER Andrew Gurza, who is in a wheelchair, shared his experience in the emergency room when he needed an exam and tests.

"I went to the doctor last year for an STI test. I hadn't been tested in a while. So I was like, 'How do I do this?' I decided to go to the local emergency room because I thought if they have to do a bigger test, take me out of my chair to do something, you know, whatever it is they have to do, they have everything there. So I go to the ER and I say, 'Hi. I would like to have an STI test.' And the nurse said, 'Why are you here for that?'

"I [say], 'Because I'm sexually active, and I'd like to have a test, please.' A couple of hours later the doctor came and saw me, and he says, 'You can just go to your GP for that.' And I said, 'Actually, my GP's office is not physically accessible to me. I can't get out of my chair in there. That's why I'm here.' The nurses didn't know how to take my blood and didn't know how to draw urine to do the test. I told them what to do, and they figured it out. But I just thought this is not how testing should go. This is not how people with a disability should be treated when they're trying to get tested. It should be accessible, and the fact that in so many places it's not accessible speaks to a huge problem with how we see people with disabilities."

*Andrew Gurza*

## COMMUNICATING FROM
## A WHEELCHAIR

A person who uses a wheelchair often experiences physical discomfort while talking with others. This is because they often have to tip their head back to make eye contact with the speaker, who is more than likely standing in front of them. Turning even slightly to face the speaker may affect the PWD's sense of balance and cause spasms. The best position is eye level, for face-to-face communication.

A deaf or deafblind person who visits the doctor's office will also have access concerns, but theirs will focus on access to information. A friend and/or sign-language interpreter will usually accompany the deaf or deafblind person to facilitate communication with medical staff.

People with intellectual and/or developmental impairments also will bring a friend or attendant to ensure that both doctor and patient have a complete understanding of the issue and care recommendations. In both cases, the PWD forfeits their personal privacy in order to consult with a medical professional.

Most blind people will require some assistance at their initial appointment in a new medical setting. Navigating becomes easier with each subsequent visit. Remember, though, that no two PWDS are the same. The examples I gave you simply illustrate challenges with access and communications within the context of health care.

Students at the Jericho Hill School for the Blind in Vancouver, BC, reading braille at their desks in 1957.

## DISABILITY AT SCHOOL

**A**s *you now know*, educational services have been provided to blind and deaf students in North America since the mid-to-late 1800s. They were delivered using the residential-school model of education, which segregates children from their families.

I attended Jericho Hill School for the Blind in Vancouver, British Columbia, in the early 1970s, for seventh and eighth grade. Prior to this I had never met a blind person. No one in my family could prepare me for this new experience, because I was the first blind person they had met. I liked the school, mostly because I was just like everyone else there.

In the early 1980s the educational system moved away from segregating disabled children in boarding schools and moved to a model of **integration**. Disabled students returned to their family homes and attended schools in their home communities. Placing one girl in an all-boys' school would not be called integration. But placing one blind or deaf student in a school of sighted students *is* considered integration. These "integrated" students often feel isolated because they lived away from home before and weren't part of the school community. I know this because I was one of those isolated "integrated" students.

Disabled students have access to supportive educational services. A blind student may have a special assistant to translate printed materials into braille. Or a deaf student may have an assistant who uses sign language to simultaneously interpret classroom conversations and instructions. Educational-resource rooms offer learning assistance to students deemed to have learning challenges. Students who are blind or deaf or have other learning disabilities have access to these supportive-learning spaces, but for some students there is a real stigma attached to being a student who needs support.

The *mainstreaming* of students remains a priority of the disabled culture, but cultural opportunities still need to be available so those students can develop a supportive peer group to complement the inclusive-education model.

# HOUSING WITH A DISABILITY FOCUS

**A** **s we learned** in chapter 2, in the past most PWDS lived with their families or were placed in institutions, often for the duration of their lives. Many of those facilities were not specifically for PWDS. They were institutions housing a blended population of prisoners and/or mentally ill patients.

*Veterans with disabilities often find that there is no place for them in society when they return home.*

With peace and greater prosperity after World War II, **warehousing** PWDS in large institutions fell out of favor, though it still happens today. Residents are often placed in institutional care facilities by family members who can no longer care for them and/or do not believe the PWD has the capacity to make good decisions about their own care.

## Housing for Veterans

Proud disabled veterans returned home from the war only to discover they could no longer function fully in regular housing because of a disability, mental-health disorder or addiction. This phenomenon continues today. According to Veterans Affairs Canada, there are between 3,000 and 5,000 homeless veterans in Canada. There are two strategies to address this issue: housing projects and individual subsidies paid directly to veterans to assist with rental costs.

After World War II, the CNIB built 25 residences and service centers across Canada for their blind clients who were not able to function independently in their own homes. Many of the residents were war-blinded veterans who were able to adapt to their disability within a safe, supportive environment designed specifically for blind people. The last CNIB residence was built in Quebec City in 1964, by which time the demand for this specialty type of housing was dwindling. The war was over, and the housing demands of war-blinded veterans decreased significantly.

## Social Housing

Social-housing complexes for PWDS and low-income Canadians became standard in Canada in the mid-1930s, following the passage of the Dominion Housing Act. Since then all levels of government have participated in establishing and managing these programs. The units are typically apartments in large rental complexes within the city. A percentage of the units are wheelchair accessible. Most people with sensory and cognitive disabilities require only a few, if any, special adaptations to their units. If money is no concern, PWDS can live in any type of accommodation they choose.

In order to live somewhat independently, PWDs may qualify for and receive help in their homes, such as an aide to provide personal and limited medical care, help with dressing, meal prep and light housekeeping. Every situation is unique, and every solution is geared to the individual's needs.

It probably sounds like this is a great service. And it is. But have you ever stopped to think about what it might feel like to have a different person perform these intensely personal tasks in your own private space? What if you didn't like one of the care aides they sent? Tough luck. When strangers are paid to assist in the tasks of daily living, PWDs may experience a disconnect between being a human and being just another body requiring cleaning, dressing and/or feeding.

## Group Homes

The *group home* became a housing option in the mid-1970s. This model consists of private houses with multiple rental rooms available to PWDS. The homes are often funded and run by nonprofit housing societies, and there is staff provided to assist with residents' care needs 24-7. The homelike, supportive atmosphere of group homes has been well received.

## Nonprofit Housing

For PWDS who prefer to live on their own but still require subsidized rent and care assistance, a third option is available. *Nonprofit housing* societies rent several apartments in regular apartment complexes. One unit is typically used as a staff room, and staff is available around the clock to provide assistance whenever a client calls in. This is a particularly cost-effective model because the housing society does not have to incur the costs of maintenance and property ownership.

Lifetime Networks, a community-support service for people with intellectual impairments, is based in Victoria, British Columbia. Lifetime Networks does not provide housing options themselves, but their clients are able to access many of the same housing options that are available to people with other kinds of disabilities. Another type of housing is a home-share option, where a client will live with a family and be part of that home environment. From time to time families are in a position to purchase a condo for use by an intellectually impaired family member. In all housing options, Lifetime Networks provides financial support and other relevant services to help clients live as successfully and independently as possible.

# —4—

# The Culture of Independence

## A DISABILITY IN THE FAMILY

**F**amily dynamics can change a lot when someone is deemed disabled. Many parents and families have had no exposure to disability and are as unaware of how to raise a disabled child as the child is unaware of what the disability will mean to their future.

If there are ongoing medical issues, the disabled child's siblings may receive less parental attention. Having a child, sister or brother with a disability doesn't instantly make you aware of what it's like to be disabled. Even our families may not feel comfortable asking us questions.

Having a disability may mean you no longer want or are able to participate in family activities you used to enjoy. Sometimes family members forget to consider how a disability might limit or impact enjoyment of an activity. Wendy Cox, who uses a wheelchair, experienced this very thing on a recent trip. She drove two hours to her family home for a get-together, only to discover that the event was going to be held on a local beach. Sandy beaches and wheelchairs do not get along—the wheels sink into the sand. Even when families are fully aware of another member's disability, they sometimes fail to think through their decisions.

Families may also incorrectly assume that their disabled child or sibling will never be able to live independently. There is often an unspoken "understanding" that someone in the family will have to assume responsibility for housing and caring for the disabled family member. My mother expected that I would live with her after I graduated from high school. My in-laws thought they would have to take care of my husband and me. I've heard similar stories from many disabled friends. We don't mean to hurt anyone's feelings, but we're as anxious as the next person to get out on our own and build lives for ourselves.

*The author and her husband, Brian, vacationing in Cozumel in 1998.*

# WITHIN OUR HOMES

**W**ithin the culture of disability, as within other groups, there are cultural norms. Our homes and the strategies we use to be as independent as possible demonstrate what is culturally normal for us. We are individuals in every way. However, we often use similar types of services and products.

For instance, the homes of most people with visual impairments will probably have numerous products with speech capabilities, such as computers, speech-activated personal assistants, talking gadgets like clocks, kitchen and bathroom scales, and audio-library collections. Almost everyone with even a small amount of vision will have a cache of magnifying glasses and electronic magnifiers. These tools are the norms in our homes, as are smartphones with various helpful apps, which you'll read about in the next chapter.

People who require *mobility aids* such as wheelchairs, walkers or canes also need distinctive items that fall into the category of cultural norms. Wheelchair users might have driving gloves to keep their hands clean. In their homes you will likely find adaptations such as a raised toilet seat, open space under bathroom and kitchen cabinets to accommodate wheelchairs, wider hallways and less clutter on the floor.

## IN REAL LIFE

**W**ENDY COX lives in a two-bedroom apartment in downtown Victoria, British Columbia, that she has shared with numerous roommates over time. She is able to independently manage activities such as cooking, cleaning, bathing and dressing. She has long, wavy hair and bemoans her inability to flat-iron the waves out of it or French-braid it herself because she has the use of only one hand. Because she manages so well, her apartment doesn't look much different than any other suite.

Wendy teaches her roommates to accommodate her in minor ways. Because she lives seated and has little strength in her hands, Wendy asks her roommates to be mindful about putting items back in the same accessible place in the kitchen and bathroom cupboards. No placing things on high shelves. No tightening lids, because of her weakened hands. And, of course, no leaving shoes and other clutter on the floor.

Wendy says that living on her own takes more time than it did before her injury. Transferring out of bed and onto the shower bench or toilet, dressing one-handed, preparing and eating breakfast add time to her morning routine before she goes off to work.

People who are able to use only one hand to dress are often frustrated by buttons, zippers, adjustable straps on shoes and more. The demand for *adaptive clothing* styles has increased as baby boomers age into disability. They often face challenges similar to those of people in wheelchairs. Limited ranges of motion make the task of dressing problematic.

Examples of adaptive clothing include Velcro-type closures instead of buttons, blouses, shirts and dresses that open in the back and use Velcro-type closures while retaining the look of traditional button styling on the front, zippers with easy-to-grasp pull tabs, and shoes with Velcro-type closures instead of shoelaces.

# TRANSPORTATION

Cars can be retrofitted to accommodate some PWDs.

Once you've established yourself in your own home with the supports you need to be independent, how do you get around the community? While some PWDS are able to drive, the majority do not and often cannot afford to either. Public transportation systems in medium-size to large cities offer wheelchair-accessible buses. Taxis are another option, as are *custom-transit services.*

Custom-transit services have fleets of wheelchair-accessible vehicles with drivers who provide a door-to-door service for PWDS unable to use the regular transit system. Many disability organizations have negotiated limited subsidized taxi services as a third option. Volunteer drivers can be a source of transportation, as long as mobility challenges are not prohibitive. Many of us are anxiously awaiting the launch of the self-driving car as yet one more transportation option. Price, of course, will pose a significant barrier to ownership.

## IN THE WORKPLACE

**W**hen I enter a grocery store, drugstore, coffee shop or clothing store, I expect to receive good customer service from the staff. I'm sure you do too. Have you ever wondered why we automatically assume that store staff will be able-bodied? Where does that assumption come from?

Look around your classroom and your school. Do any of the teachers use a wheelchair to get around? Maybe a guide dog? Do any of the support staff have disabilities? Ask your parents and other adult relatives if they work alongside anyone with a disability. I don't know you or where you live, but I can predict your response. I can predict it because I have lived with my visual impairment almost my entire life and have always struggled with finding meaningful mainstream employment—as have my peers.

I'm also qualified to talk to you on this subject because I've had numerous part- and full-time jobs since starting my first summer job in my teens. I've had a lot of experiences, good and bad, and I'm not alone in that regard. The statistics back me up.

When it comes to finding employment, the statistics are abysmal for PWDS. According to Statistics Canada, there is a staggering 55 percent unemployment rate among PWDS aged 25 to 65. The unemployment rate for blind people is above 80 percent.

The 2016–17 United States Bureau of Labor Statistics reported that only 18.7 percent of PWDS are employed. This means 81.3 percent of Americans with a disability are not employed. It's hard to summon the courage to launch a job search in the face of such daunting statistics.

All levels of government have tried to address this problem, in their own ways and at different times. It's complicated. There is no one-program-fits-all solution to the high unemployment rates among PWDS. Educational levels vary. Accessible transportation may be an issue. The workplace may not be accessible. Not everyone has the capacity to compete in today's demanding workplace either. And then there's the matter of the people themselves.

**81.3 percent of Americans with a disability are not employed.**

The late Dr. Kenneth Jernigan, former president of the National Federation of the Blind (NFB), was right on the money when he said, "We who are blind are pretty much like you. We have our share of both geniuses and jerks, but most of us are somewhere between, ordinary people living ordinary lives." Yes, there are geniuses and jerks in every community. Why would that be any different for PWDS?

The most common employment initiative is to offer incentives to employers. Governments want to make it beneficial for a potential employer to hire someone with a disability. The program might partially subsidize wages for a time, assist with funding an accessible workplace, if needed, and provide funding for *adaptive technology* where required. The goal of the *incentive program* is to entice employers to give persons with disabilities a chance to prove they can be a real asset in the workplace while minimizing the financial risk to the employer. In theory, it makes sense.

Many such programs often run just long enough for the disabled employee to qualify for employment insurance, and then the worker must start the job-search process all over again. These programs give the employers a chance to witness the competence and capacity of disabled workers while giving the workers much-needed experience. Employment incentive programs are not without benefits. They do, however, suggest that PWDs need to be subsidized in the workplace because they're not comparable to able-bodied staff.

As Martin Luther King Jr., the legendary American civil-rights leader, once said, "We are stuck in the esthetics of equity." Employment incentive programs make it appear as though PWDs are employable and employed, but we seldom hear what happens when the incentive funding runs out. My first job was through a funding program, and so was the last one I accepted some 35 years later.

## IN REAL LIFE

**E**NTREPRENEURS WITH DISABILITIES is a self-employment initiative for PWDs in rural communities throughout Saskatchewan and Manitoba. Taylor Leighton of Outlook, Saskatchewan, is the latest recipient of funding assistance for her rural recycling program.

Taylor is a young woman with an intellectual impairment who is passionate about recycling. She started her business with neighbors and family members as her first customers. But thanks to the program, she has now developed a lucrative business, according to Taylor's mother, who helps out with driving once a week. Taylor's mother is proud of her daughter's initiative and believes self-employment is the best option for Taylor because the traditional workplace is too competitive for her.

*If you work for yourself, you won't need to convince an employer you can do the job despite your disability.*

Now that is the definition of stuck! Some disabled people choose to go another route to avoid the confidence-crushing experiences of the job-search process.

Self-employment is another option. Professions such as physiotherapy, counseling, massage therapy and piano tuning are examples of fields in which self-employment has worked for decades for a number of blind and visually impaired people.

College-level career-training programs often offer co-op employment opportunities for disabled students. This is a great way to get some experience and network

## IN REAL LIFE

**SCOTT LABARRE** practises law in Denver, Colorado. In addition to operating his own law office, Scott works at the NFB as a disability-rights lawyer. You probably think that Scott, as a professional person, has access to multiple job opportunities. Think again. Scott says, "The job search was really frustrating. Most of my able friends would just send out their résumés and get multiple offers of employment. I had to scrap and scrape and fight for opportunities." Further, he says, as president of the National Association of Blind Lawyers he knows that the same holds true today. Blind law students and legal professionals struggle much more to get the same opportunities in the legal field as do their able-bodied legal peers.

## IN REAL LIFE

**E**MPLOYMENT FOR PWDS is a complicated, challenging issue. There are employment success stories, but they are the exception, not the rule. We need to come up with innovative ideas and actions, because the current system isn't working.

One young woman is breaking the mold when it comes to going where no mobility-challenged woman has gone before.

Tiphany Adams was born in California. In 2000, at age 17, she was the sole survivor of a head-on collision with a drunk driver. The accident left her to experience the world in a wheelchair. Tiphany is a model and actor. She was one of four young women in wheelchairs who participated in a reality-TV show entitled *Push Girls*. She challenges the world of fashion to reject her great looks, intelligence and positive attitude.

*Tiphany Adams*

with potential employers. The general consensus is to specialize. If you work for yourself, you won't need to convince an employer you can do the job despite your disability.

PWDS who go into social work, psychology, teaching and law often provide services through their own disability-specific agencies because professionals in these fields, despite a postsecondary education, are often ill-informed when it comes to the abilities of PWDS.

Chiara Bordi at a modeling shoot, showing her crystal-encrusted prosthesis.

According to an online article called "20 Disabled Models and How They Got Their Starts," models with disabilities are letting their images speak for themselves. Numerous models featured in the piece have suffered partial arm and leg amputations, and others are using their modeling careers as platforms to speak out about their autism and Down syndrome. They all expressed concern that they want to be hired as models in their own right, not simply because they are disabled.

Speaking of looks, let's talk about physical appearance within the PWD population. I used to think that more education would be the secret to fitting in socially and getting a job. I thoroughly enjoyed the university experience, but it didn't seem to change the outcome of my efforts in the job market. I attended résumé-writing workshops, took interview-skills training and researched and shopped for the best interview look I could find. Many years later, I still find myself wondering if it's the way I look that has hindered my job searches.

Most of us know the importance of making a positive first impression. When we attend a job interview, we usually have the jitters. We enter the interview space, take a seat, retrieve a copy of our résumé from our portfolio, along with a list of questions, and wait for the interview to begin.

I do all these things, but in my case it also means navigating a totally unfamiliar space while trying to look calm, cool and collected. I don't know the layout of the room so am shown to a chair. I have

> Many years later, I still find myself wondering if it's the way I look that has hindered my job searches.

to get my guide dog settled before I pluck my résumé from my portfolio. I still don't understand the physical layout of the space. Four different voices introduce themselves to me from varying locations around a long boardroom-style table.

Once the questions start, I give my best responses, attempting to appear as though I'm looking right at the questioner. But I can only look in the vicinity of their voice, as they are just a blurry form to me. The voice at the far end of the table poses an additional challenge. His blurry shape is so far away it blends into the environment. Where do I look to respond to his question? I strain my eyes, trying to make out the shape that is his voice, but then I'm distracted momentarily because straining to see out of my one good eye causes my other, not-so-good eye to wander. At least, I'm told it does. I can't tell what it's doing, so there I am, trying to formulate and deliver an intelligent response while being unable to see the questioners and while stressing about whether my eye is wandering and making me look, well, weird.

> *I can only look in the vicinity of their voice, as they are just a blurry form to me.*

Other than my wandering eye, I look pretty much what you'd call normal. What about people who don't? How do interviewers truly react to applicants with only one arm or leg, or no arms or no legs at all? What about someone who has spasticity problems that are worse when they are under pressure, like, say, in a job interview? What if the applicant stutters or slurs their words, making communication difficult? How much do our looks and our *otherness* affect the interview outcome? I'm convinced that PWDS with less-severe forms of disability, who look the most like the interviewers, tend to be more successful in the job market.

Tony Giles

"It was nine days of magic. I touched whale bones washed up on the shore, sat on huge chunks of ice, stroked glaciers and listened to the cackles of penguins all around."

# TRAVEL

**'ve done a lot** of public speaking about visual impairment, at elementary schools, high schools and colleges. Afterward there's always a question-and-answer period. One day a young woman in training to be a dental hygienist asked me, "What do you do to feel free?"

What do I do to feel free? Hmm. She elaborated that lots of able-bodied graduating students travel to Europe, go on backpacking journeys, things like that. She wondered whether people with disabilities are able to enjoy similar rites of passage through travel. I am pleased to say that yes, we are able to travel, providing, of course, that we have the funds to do so.

You may wonder why a blind person would want to travel. I'm not the person to answer that question, but Tony Giles is. Not only is he totally blind, but he has also lost 80 percent of his hearing. Despite these challenges, he has been to 124 countries thus far in his career as a wanderer. Here is one example of how he experiences travel with only his senses of touch, smell and taste to inform him.

Sharing a snippet from his trip to Antarctica, he reports, "It was nine days of magic. I touched whale bones washed up on the shore, sat on huge chunks of ice, stroked glaciers and listened to the cackles of penguins all around." Tony prefers train and ship travel to airplanes because he receives more *haptic* information about his environment through the motion they make.

For those of us who aren't quite as courageous as Tony, there are more structured ways to experience travel. I haven't given international travel much consideration because I would need someone to be a guide/partner. That level of dependency puts a strain on even the best of friendships. Besides, it would be no fun to feel that I might be restricting my companion's plans because I can't be

*The author in Paris in 2003.*

independent in a completely foreign environment where language might be an additional barrier.

Traveleyes is a UK-based international tour operator with a difference. Launched in 2004 by blind entrepreneur Amar Latif, Traveleyes offers exciting world-travel opportunities for blind and visually impaired people from all over the world. Tour groups are

Traveleyes founder, Amar Latif.

small, between 14 and 20 people. Half the travelers are blind or visually impaired and half are fully sighted. Blind travelers pay full price while sighted travelers pay approximately half that, because they have signed on to be guides. Each day a sighted traveler is paired with a different blind traveler. Changing partners on a daily basis means that everyone gets to know everyone else. Blind travelers tell their sighted friends how much they can see and how they like to be guided. Then it's off to explore! The best part is that because the company is focused on the needs of blind travelers, it often can arrange for special, up-close access to experiences such as safaris and the Terracotta Army in China.

Aufgang Travel, located in Toronto, Ontario, is another agency that specializes in providing international travel opportunities for persons with disabilities. Whether you want to cruise or be part of a land tour, this agency provides specialty services upon request. Individual or group tours can be set up.

Cruising has become popular among PWDS, since cruise ships are typically wheelchair accessible. It's simple to get around once you've figured out the layout. There are relieving areas for guide dogs aboard ship. Such accommodations make for a welcoming, inclusive experience.

The airline industry is able to accommodate disabled travelers as well. Because of limited space, people who use wheelchairs may be required to place them in the cargo hold during the flight. Service dogs are permitted on board. Some airlines now provide an additional seat for the dog at no extra cost. The dog doesn't actually take the seat—it's the floor space in front of the empty seat that's for the dog. This makes the flight much more comfortable for the dog, and it gives the dog's handler a bit more leg room. Prior to this change, the dog

was required to curl up in front of the owner's seat, leaving the handler with almost no space for their feet. This extra-seat policy is available only on Canadian airlines.

The travel industry has mostly been accepting of disabled travelers and the adaptations we require. Customer-service training with the needs of PWDs at the forefront has resulted in a better understanding of the service needs of this population. With myriad assistive mobility devices, problems with proper handling do occur from time to time, resulting in dings and dents and battery damage. But with more and more PWDs opting to travel, services can only improve, right?

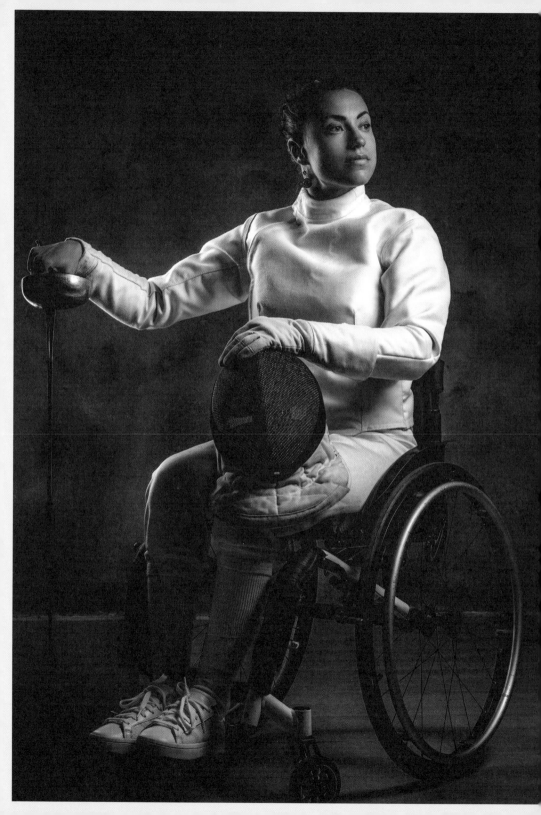

# SPORTS AND RECREATION

**I**n most communities today, recreational opportunities for PWDS abound. So do volunteer services. People with sensory disabilities may need assistance with activities such as cycling, playing golf, skiing, curling, water sports and fitness programs, to name a few. Those with physical disabilities are first and foremost concerned with their ability to access facilities. They may want to engage the services of a friend or volunteer as an assistant.

## Golf

Blind golfers use the services of an assistant who can describe in detail the requirements of the next shot. Golf requires good body awareness and a strong stance and swing. These are physical actions. A person doesn't really need to see to swing the club. Besides, golfers don't look at the ball on the tee. They simply know it's there.

Disabled golfers have many opportunities to compete in their sport at local, regional and national levels. The International Blind Golf Association has sponsored tournaments for blind golfers since its inception in 1998. The association reports that it has some 500 blind golfers on its ever-increasing membership list.

*Derek Kibblewhite and sight coach Chris Chambers get lined up for their first tee shot at the 2017 ISPS Handa Vision Cup in Creston, BC.*

## Curling

Adaptive curling is now available to people with sensory disabilities as well as those in wheelchairs. Curlers with vision challenges are assisted by a guide who can describe where the rocks are and what kind of shots are called for. To help the player line up their shot, the guide may hold the broom a short distance in front of them or use a flashlight to show the line of the delivery. People who are totally blind are guided by the coach's voice. Other than lining up for the shot, the rest of the game is the same as it is for able-bodied players.

People in wheelchairs have taken to curling in a big way. They position themselves for the shot, focus on the broom at the other end of the ice, push forward and release the rock with the aid of a delivery stick, a piece of equipment new to the game of curling. It was first developed because elderly curlers found it increasingly difficult to crouch down and slide out for the delivery. The stick has made it possible for them and people who use wheelchairs to participate in the game.

## Skiing

Downhill and cross-country skiing are also popular activities for many PWDs. Blind skiers use the services of a guide partner to communicate course information to them while skiing. And if you watch the Winter Paralympics, you'll see physically challenged athletes taking on the slopes with only one leg or only one arm or sometimes no legs at all. Double-leg amputees enjoy a modified form of skiing called sit-skiing. The sit-ski was one of the first sitting-position sleds developed for people with lower-extremity limitations.

For many PWDs who skied prior to their injuries, adaptations such as the sit-ski allow them to return to the sport they love in a different way. The imperative to feel their body flying down the slopes again is worth the risk that comes with this activity.

## Hockey

Para ice hockey, also known as sledge hockey, is a modified form of the game for physically disabled people. The player sits on a sled equipped with blades and carries a stick in each hand. Each stick has a pick at one end, which players use to propel their sled along the surface of the ice, and a hooked blade at the other end for handling the puck.

## IN REAL LIFE

**I**N APRIL 2018 tragedy struck Saskatchewan's Humboldt Broncos when the bus carrying the hockey team to a playoff game collided with a transport truck. Sixteen people were killed and 13 were seriously injured. Two of the survivors, Ryan Straschnitzki and Jacob Wassermann, were paralyzed because of the accident. But when you're a hockey player at heart, there's not much that can keep you off the ice. Only seven months after their surgeries and rehabilitation, these two players took to the ice again.

Ryan says when he woke up to discover the extent of his injuries, his first thought was that he'd never be able to play hockey again, that he'd never feel the ease and speed of skating across the ice. But sledge hockey made it possible for him to revisit the thrill of hockey again. His goal is to participate in the sport at the Paralympic level.

Visually impaired hockey players enjoy the sport as well. Two simple adaptations—a slightly larger and slower, beeping hockey puck and lower hockey nets—force players to keep the puck/play at ice level to reduce possible injuries.

## At the Beach

For lots of people, summertime means spending time at the beach, feeling the warm sand between their toes and maybe doing a little swimming with friends and family. To someone who uses a wheelchair or walker, summertime means not being able to enjoy the beach because the wheels of wheelchairs and the legs of walkers sink into the sand. What's a beach-loving PWD to do?

*Mobi-Mats allow people who use wheelchairs to spend time on the beach.*

The Mobi-Mat is the solution. The mat is a portable, lightweight, nonslip roll-out beach access pathway for individuals of all abilities, whether they are walking or using a wheelchair, stroller, bicycle or ATV. The Mobi-Mat was originally developed for desert warfare, as a solution for army vehicles getting stuck in the sand. It's a good example of an innovation with numerous applications. The company that makes the mat also sells a floating wheelchair.

———

Think of any recreational activity. There's probably someone out there with a disability who is participating in that very activity, even if they need volunteer assistance and slight adaptations. The next time you're out with your friends at a recreation center, softball field or tennis court, stop and think about how someone with a disability could join in too, how they could be on the team alongside able-bodied friends and neighbors. Blind people do play a version of softball using a baseball that beeps. Blind tennis enthusiasts in Japan developed a large foam tennis ball that's easier to see and hear. Surprised? You should know by now that if PWDs want to do something, they'll find a way.

# TAKING IT TO THE NEXT LEVEL

*n both Canada* and the United States, government assistance is available to elite disabled athletes to assist with their living and training expenses. Athletes who receive funding are called *carded athletes*. As funding recipients, they must maintain a set performance level as set out in the assistance fund.

## Wheelchair Basketball

This sport came into being after World War II as a key part of rehabilitating war-injured veterans. It was one of eight sports for PWDS featured at the 1960 Olympics. The 1968 Olympics featured the first-ever women's wheelchair basketball team. In addition to participating in the Olympics and Paralympics, wheelchair basketball teams can compete in the World Wheelchair Basketball Championship, which has been held every four years since the first one in Belgium in 1975.

*South Africa plays Japan in the 2017 Men's U23 World Wheelchair Basketball Championship in Toronto, ON.*

*Team Australia and Team Japan compete for the gold medal in the Wheelchair Rugby World Championships in 2018.*

## Wheelchair Rugby, or Murderball

In order to play wheelchair basketball, players must have upper-body strength as well as the ability to use their hands and arms. Where does that leave those with limited upper-body strength who want to be involved with team sports? Well, it leaves them on the murderball court.

Known as quad rugby in the United States, murderball is a co-ed game played on a basketball court by athletes in reinforced wheelchairs. Conceived by five Canadian men with *quadriplegia*, the game is a blend of wheelchair basketball, rugby and handball. It is also the most popular event at the Paralympics. At the 2012 Games, murderball drew a sell-out crowd of 12,000 spectators, who cheered and roared while the four players on each team crashed and smashed into one another to prevent scoring. This sport is not for the faint of heart.

Other sporting options for PWDs include wheelchair tennis, soccer and baseball. The lone-wolf sports fan can try motocross, mountain biking and/or surfing. It's no longer a matter of *if* you can do a particular sport or activity as a PWD, but *when* you will do it.

I'm still trying to come up with an answer to the question about what I do to feel free. My deafblind friend Penny decided to figure out whether tandem skydiving would give her that feeling of freedom.

Reflecting on her first successful jump, Penny says, "The thing I love is [that] most people haven't skydived. Usually I'm the one who doesn't know something they know. Having skydived when most haven't gives me that unusual feeling of…not superiority, maybe just being in a position of knowledge and experience that most others haven't had. It's a very liberating feeling."

## ARTS AND ENTERTAINMENT

*didn't used to* be a fan of television. The action was too visual for me. I missed body-language cues that add layers of meaning to scenes. It was frustrating. Now I watch Channel 888, AMI-TV. AMI stands for Accessible Media Inc. The channel offers descriptive audio on all its programming. During ads and programs, a background voice provides critical information about scenery and facial expressions, as well as explanations of action scenes. I love it. I don't feel like I'm missing anything.

Then there's the matter of live theater. Blind and visually impaired people haven't typically been able to fully enjoy the theater scene. While we can follow the dialogue in the play, it's easy to miss the physical action. Scenery and costumes also add a lot to the enjoyment

of a play. It wasn't until the concept of described theater came to town that I was able to enjoy the theater experience too.

"Good afternoon, and welcome to VocalEye's described performance of *Goodnight Desdemona (Good Morning Juliet)* by Ann-Marie MacDonald, directed by Ron Jenkins and produced by the Belfry Theatre. I'm Steph Kirkland, and I'll be your describer for today." Steph's voice in my wireless headphones guided me through my first described-theater experience.

It was similar to watching TV on the AMI channel, but better. Check out this description.

*Janitor mops floor, smokes cigarette.*

*One hand on mop.*

*Lets go of mop—the handle remains upright.*

I laughed along with other audience members, sharing a comedic moment in real time. What a treat not to have to tap a friend on the shoulder and whisper, "What just happened there? Why is everyone laughing?" I was hooked.

Persons with hearing loss use live interpreter services to enhance the theatre experience, while people using wheelchairs and/or walkers are able to access exclusive seating designed to comfortably accommodate the additional space they require.

Whether it's in travel or sports or the arts, the collective voice of PWDs and their supporters continues to create more awareness and availability of inclusive and accessible recreational opportunities for everyone.

## DATING IN THE DIGITAL AGE

**S**ocial media offers so many ways for people to meet. There are websites exclusively for persons with disabilities, including *Dating4Disabled, Whispers4u, Disabled Passions* and *Special Bridge*. These sites offer the typical services of any online dating site.

## MARRIAGE AND PARENTING

**A** *few weeks after* I married Brian, who was also visually impaired, my mother told me about a comment my aunt had made at the reception. "It's a good thing their kind sticks together," she said. Bless my dear old auntie's ignorant heart. Did she honestly believe we disabled people would pose a threat to the human race if we intermarried with sighted people? I wondered what she thought about the three—count 'em, three—people in wheelchairs at our wedding. Unfortunately, this (usually) silent belief about disabled people marrying and having children is not uncommon.

*The Atlantic* recently released a short documentary called *The Right to Sexuality*, which follows the hurdles a married couple had to clear to convince a group home to allow them to live together. They both have intellectual disabilities, but that doesn't mean they are incapable of understanding their sexuality or being in a marital relationship. The couple had to legally prove that they could consent to their sexual relationship and thereby earn their right to live together. The mere fact that the couple had to go through

> ## WHAT DOES INTERABLED MEAN?
>
> *Interabled* is an adjective that describes a relationship in which one person has a disability and the other does not.

this process speaks volumes about the social and cultural perception of the sexuality of people with disabilities.

I couldn't find statistics on the number of people with disabilities who marry and/or choose to have a family. In all cultural groups, some people choose to marry within their culture and others choose to look outside their culture for a life partner. The same holds true for PWDS.

I chose to marry Brian, a man with a visual impairment. I admit I feel more comfortable being with someone who also has an intimate understanding of the challenges vision loss poses. But that's just me. Others prefer to partner with people who are able-bodied and able to ease some of those challenges.

But choosing to marry an able-bodied person or another disabled person isn't necessarily a conscious choice we make. Chemistry happens when it happens. PWDS probably spend more social time with other PWDS, the way you probably spend most of your social time with people you feel comfortable with too.

## Bringing Up Baby

Deciding to have a family can be daunting. First-time parents often feel overwhelmed by the demands of having a baby. It is no different for a PWD. Pregnancy and childbirth may present extra physical challenges and possible complications for women with disabilities. That's why it's critical to find a supportive physician, someone who has some experience with and understanding of the disabled body.

## IN REAL LIFE

**D**EAF MOTHER ELIZABETH EDGAR is a stay-at-home parent and blogger living in Florida. Her blog, *Mommy Gone Tropical*, is about her experiences as a deaf parent of two hearing children. Her husband, Mr. Tropical, is also a deaf parent. Edgar enthusiastically shares her advice on how deaf parents can know when their babies are crying.

Edgar's favorite technology is the Sonic Alert baby-cry signaler paired with the Sonic Alert alarm clock. The clock makes the bed vibrate when it goes off. When the clock is paired with the signaler, the entire bed vibrates when the signaler is activated. According to Edgar, her husband has a hard time going back to sleep if the entire bed vibrates, so she uses a secondary alarm attachment, a pillow vibrator, so Mr. Tropical can sleep.

In addition, Edgar recommends an infant video monitor. She clips this unit to her shirt, and it vibrates when the baby starts to fuss and/or cry. She also uses her phone to monitor the baby when she is in a different part of their home. She uses the FaceTime app in conjunction with a tablet, placed with the screen facing the baby in the crib, to keep her baby in constant view. She, like many other deaf parents, uses personal resources and technology to help her care for her baby.

Those of us who have only a sensory disability and no fertility issues typically have uncomplicated pregnancies. This may not be the case for someone with a spinal-cord injury, who uses a wheelchair. When you're unable to dash to a bathroom, morning sickness can be an almost-daily complication for the first trimester of the pregnancy. As mom and baby grow, the mother's sense of balance is affected by the shifting weight increase and distribution.

Each disability poses a unique challenge to the person having a baby. Blind people can hear the baby crying and can feel if the baby has a temperature, but they may not notice a mild case of diaper rash. The most common question deaf parents are asked is how they know when their baby is crying.

Creative thinking and technology work well together to create solutions for parents with disabilities. Unfortunately, not enough people know that PWDs can and do parent effectively all the time. This lack of knowledge, especially on the part of public health staff, has resulted in the wrongful apprehension of children of disabled parents, based solely on the erroneous belief that PWDs lack the capacity to parent well.

According to Bonnie Brayton, the executive director of DisAbled Women's Network of Canada (DAWN), "Even today, disabled mothers are often told that having children will worsen their conditions, that their disabilities will be passed on to their children and that they won't be competent mothers."

"When they do have children, the majority of parents with disabilities have a fear of their children being apprehended, because you know you are being watched—right, wrong or otherwise," says Melanie Moore, who works with disabled parents at the Centre for Independent Living in Toronto (CILT) in Ontario.

Comprehensive statistics are not available on the number of children who are apprehended from their family homes because authorities decided that people with disabilities can't possibly parent effectively. Disabled-parenting advocates have rallied for changes, but stereotypes persist.

The National Federation of the Blind (NFB) in the United States developed a reference booklet on parenting with a disability, which it makes available to human-services professionals. Disability-parenting organizations are plentiful and easy to access now with social media. When apprehensions occur, the word gets out quickly, and advocacy groups go to work.

The NFB has lobbied state governments to appeal laws allowing apprehension of minor children based simply on parental disability. As of summer 2019, according to the NFB legal department, 14 states can no longer apprehend a child solely because a parent has a disability.

Living well with a disability has its rewards and difficulties, but parents with disabilities should not have to live with the fear of having their child apprehended because the authorities possess all the power but limited or no awareness of the successful lifestyle practices of PWDS.

# DISABILITIES IN THE LGBTQ+ COMMUNITY

*LGBTQ+ PWDs participate in the Pride parade in Kyiv, Ukraine, in 2019.*

**U**nderstanding your gender identity can be challenging for anyone, disabled or not. It wasn't until its 2018 annual general meeting that the NFB welcomed its first-ever formal contingent of LGBTQ+ members. Yes, 2018, almost eight decades after the NFB's inception in 1940. Both the disability and LGBTQ+ communities may have some work to do regarding inclusiveness as well.

June has been recognized as Pride Month since the Stonewall Inn riots of June 1969. In June 2019, the 50th anniversary of the riots, Sarah Kim wrote an article for *Forbes* online, entitled "Pride Month Too Often Overlooks LGBTQ+ Members with Disabilities," in which she calls for the LGBTQ+ community to be more inclusive.

Kim, who identifies as a trans disabled woman, says, "Disability accommodations and inclusivity should not be an afterthought, but rather a priority when planning LGBTQ+ events and celebrations."

Is it unreasonable to expect everyone in every business, social or recreational situation to demonstrate a high level of knowledge about disabilities? I pose this question in my role as an *other,* who has been taught to graciously accept "good enough" and not make a fuss.

# —5—

# Engineering a Brighter Future with Technology

**S**martphones, smart homes, virtual personal assistants and artificial intelligence (AI), combined with smartphone apps, play a larger and larger role in the lives of PWDs every day and will no doubt continue to increase in popularity. The same type of *accessibility* issues that PWDs are confronted with in transit, employment, housing and recreation also exist in the area of technology. But while there are stumbling blocks in the day-to-day use of communication technologies, this same field has produced life-changing products and services for disabled people.

The goal of advancing technologies is to enhance products and services with respect to safety, independence and discretion for PWDS, but before we talk about high tech, let's look at some of the things that PWDS have been using for years.

# FOR THE BLIND AND VISUALLY IMPAIRED

## The White Cane

We understand the purpose of a cane when it is used for support, but most people don't understand how the same cane, painted white, mysteriously becomes a navigational tool for a blind person. The white cane was introduced between the world wars, and although low-tech in nature, it has allowed blind people to move about their environments with relative safety.

Without a cane, the only way a blind person can truly know what is in front or to either side of them is to feel around them—to literally touch the ground and other objects. When I received my first white cane, I didn't want to use it because I thought people might pity me because I'm blind. But what would they think if I was down on my hands and knees, feeling my way around? Now that is hardly dignified behavior.

The long white cane works as an extension of my fingertip "eyes." I hold the cane in my right hand, extend it in front of me for its length and allow the tip of the cane to make contact with the ground. By moving the tip of the cane in a repetitive right-to-left and left-to-right arc motion in front of me, I can deduce a number of things.

1.  What kind of surface am I on?
2.  Is the surface level?
3.  Am I walking in a straight line?

There are all kinds of tips and tricks used by blind people to get around safely with a white cane. An instructor in the field of orientation and mobility (O&M) teaches newly blind people how to effectively use this tool.

## Guide and Service Dogs

After noting how well his German shepherd assisted blind war veterans in his hospital, Dr. Gerhard Stalling opened the world's first guide-dog school in Germany in 1916. Soon there were other schools for training dogs for service.

*A statue of Morris Frank and his seeing-eye dog, Buddy, in Morristown, NJ.*

Dorothy Harrison Eustis

One of the people impressed by what these schools were doing was Dorothy Harrison Eustis, who bred and trained German shepherds in Switzerland. She wrote an article about the German guide dogs that was read to Morris Frank, a young blind man from Tennessee. He traveled to Switzerland to work with Eustis and a service dog he named Buddy. Their successful work with Buddy led to their co-founding the United States' first guide-dog school in 1929. The Seeing Eye was relocated to Morristown, New Jersey, in 1965, where it continues to operate to this day.

From time to time I hear people refer to my dog as a *seeing-eye dog*. That's not entirely correct. The generic name is *guide dog* or *service dog*. Because the Seeing Eye was the first and only school in North America for many years, the term *guide dog* became synonymous with *seeing-eye dog*.

As of 2019, there were 16 guide-dog training centers in the United States and five in Canada. Schools estimate that there are approximately 10,000 dog-and-handler teams in North America today. I am pleased

**I don't feel so much of an other when I'm with my dog, Ogden.**

to say I am one of those dog-and-handler teams. I don't feel so much of an *other* when I'm with my dog, Ogden. People talk to us on the bus and in stores and restaurants. They want to know all about him. Nobody ever asked me about my cane or gushed over how cute it was.

The author with her first guide dog, Calvin, a standard poodle who was also hypoallergenic.

As long as Ogden remains healthy, I expect he will work until he is 10 or 11 years old. When he retires, I have the option to either keep him as a pet or find another home for him.

It is against the law to refuse a guide dog entrance to any business or public facility. He goes wherever I go. Here are the dos and don'ts when you are around a service animal of any kind:

> **RULE #1:** *Don't pet a working dog. Why? Because it's working. You'll distract it from its job. Dog handlers will tell you that the most frequently used phrase they hear is "I know I'm not supposed to pet your dog, but…" If you know you're not supposed to, don't.*

> **RULE #2:** *Please don't feed a guide dog. Why? Because it's working. You'll distract it from its job. You wouldn't go over to a paramedic who's trying to revive someone with CPR and offer her an ice-cream cone, would you? Why? Because she's working. You'll distract her from her job.*

> **RULE #3:** *Do not engage with the guide dog by making eye contact or smiling at it. Why? Because it's working. You'll distract it from its job.*

> **RULE #4:** *Always follow rules 1 through 3.*

## Audible Crosswalk Signals

Prior to audible signals, blind people were taught to listen for the different sounds and directions of traffic surges to help them assess whether it was safe to cross. Audible signals are commonplace in major cities today. A blind pedestrian simply has to stop at the curb, locate the post, push the button and wait for the audible signal to know when it's safe to cross.

The signals have a dual purpose. Not only do they increase safety, but they also provide vital directional information. The cuckoo signal indicates it's safe for pedestrians to cross in a north-south direction. The chirp signal indicates it's safe to cross in an east-west direction.

## Audiobooks

Thanks to Thomas Edison's 1877 invention of a way to record the human voice *and* play it back, experimentation with recording books for the blind began. The first reference to recorded talking books is in 1932. The audiobook has evolved from those early vinyl long-playing records (LPS) to cassette tapes to digital audio formats.

Audiobooks have their limitations though. For example, it is next to impossible to find a specific page or section of text, highlight text or make notations in the margin. For me, the most profound implication of the audio format is that I never hear my own voice inside my head as I listen. I feel once removed from the reading experience, but I still love, love, love books.

## Braille

Braille isn't as mysterious as people think, and it's pretty easy to learn too. I learned it when I was 10, so how hard can it be? Here's a quick lesson.

*People who know braille can use it to read mathematical equations, scientific and musical notations as well as text.*

Braille is a system of raised dots. Each collection of six dots is called a braille cell. Using these six dots, which are arranged in two parallel rows, I can read and write every word ever created.

The dots can also be used to express mathematical equations and do scientific notations. And if that's not impressive enough for you, these same six dots are used for musical notation as well.

**Braille Alphabet**

As you can see in the braille alphabet chart, numerous combinations of the six dots are used to create letters and symbols. As with learning most everything, eventually the alphabet becomes so embedded in memory that you no longer have to think about the formation of each letter or symbol as you read.

Braille is usually typed using a machine called a manual Perkins brailler. Technology has improved on my old manual brailler over the years.

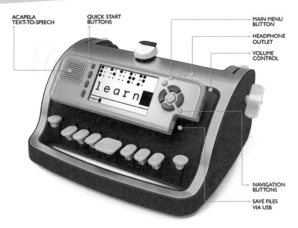

This book was written on a Perkins SMART brailler similar to this one.

ACAPELA
TEXT-TO-SPEECH

QUICK START
BUTTONS

MAIN MENU
BUTTON

HEADPHONE
OUTLET

VOLUME
CONTROL

NAVIGATION
BUTTONS

SAVE FILES
VIA USB

I now have a unit that is equivalent to a laptop, except that it has a braille keyboard instead of a regular keyboard, and one line of braille output instead of a screen. This unit has pretty much everything I need—a word processor, a calculator, a spreadsheet, email and internet. Best of all, the files are digital, so there's no paper to deal with. Even though I enter content using a braille keyboard, I can save files as Word documents and print them directly off this unit.

## Money, Money, Money

Even something as simple as handling financial affairs has changed for people with visual disabilities. Coins are always easy to identify because they each feel different. But how does a blind person tell one bill from another? In the past there was no universal rule to mark paper money. Each person devised their own meaningful method. I used simple origami practices to identify the denomination of each bill.

The Bank of Canada no longer produces traditional paper money. Canadian bills are now made of polymer and cannot be folded.

The Bank of Canada now makes currency with people with visual disabilities in mind.

Fortunately, folks at the bank thought of people with visual disabilities when the new notes were designed. The numbers on the bills are larger and bolder than ever before. The bank also incorporated a tactile element on the notes, similar to but not braille.

American bills do not yet have a tactile element, but the iBill Talking Banknote Identifier is now available free of charge from the US Department of the Treasury for any American citizen who is blind or visually impaired.

The banking industry has also learned a lot about the needs of their disabled clients when it comes to service delivery. ATMs are now at a height that is accessible to someone in a wheelchair. Most ATMs today have voice output too. If you want privacy, you need to take a pair of headphones with you to listen as you enter your information.

Online banking is also accessible to blind and visually impaired people who use screen-reading software. I've used four different bank sites in the last number of years, and I was really pleased with how easy they were to navigate.

Tap technology while shopping is a huge bonus for PWDs too. Instead of manually finding the scanner, inserting the card and asking the cashier to read the screen for me before I enter the info, I just tap. For people with limited hand movements, the tap function makes transactions a lot simpler.

*Imagine having to hold this up to your ear to hear!*

# FOR THE DEAF AND HARD OF HEARING

## Hearing Aids

The deaf and hard-of-hearing community has also gained immeasurably from advocacy and technology over the years. Humankind's first attempt to address hearing loss was the ear trumpet, which collected sound waves and led them into the ear.

The invention of the telephone and the discovery of electricity allowed for the development of the first hearing aids. The carbon transmitter and vacuum tubes demonstrated that amplification was possible, but it wasn't until 1932 that the first wearable hearing aids were available. They required battery packs, which were large and bulky.

In 1948 transistors were developed, and in 1953 the combination of vacuum-tube technology and transistors made it possible to engineer smaller, wearable hearing aids.

By 2005 digital technology had taken over the hearing-aid market. Digital technology allows for hearing aids customized to the wearer's needs, something that was never possible before.

*Cochlear implants have revolutionized the lives of profoundly deaf or severely hard-of-hearing people.*

## Cochlear Implants

The greatest-ever leap in hearing-loss technology is the **cochlear implant**. This is a small, complex electronic device that can help provide a sense of sound to a person who is profoundly deaf or severely hard of hearing. At a cost of approximately US$60,000, the device consists of three parts. An external portion sits behind the ear and captures sound signals—a sound processor. The second part is a receiver, which is surgically implanted under the skin just in front of the ear. The sound processor sends the signals to the receiver, which transmits them to the third part of the implant, electrodes implanted in the inner ear (cochlea).

Cochlear implants create vibrational representations of sound. The deaf person must learn what these sounds represent. It isn't hearing as we hearing people know it. To date the implant cannot differentiate between male and female voices, but advancements in this area continue.

# CLOSED-CAPTIONING

*Closed-captioning*, or text subtitling, allows deaf and hard-of-hearing people to watch television or movies without having to rely on reading the lips of the actors. Actors often turn away from the camera, and background sounds might indicate actions the hearing-impaired person couldn't know about.

There are two types of closed-captioning—prerecorded and real time. Court reporters are able to record the spoken words during a show because they are trained to capture up to 225 words per minute. During real-time captioning, the viewer waits only two to three seconds to see the text on screen. The first use of regularly scheduled closed-captioning was in the United States in 1980. When the Americans with Disabilities Act was passed in 1990, all public venues were required to provide closed-captioning information for audio announcements as well. Various pieces of US legislation continue to improve the quality of this service.

In Canada, the Canadian Radio-Television and Telecommunications Commission implemented closed-captioning only after the disability rights movement identified the need for it.

## American Sign Language (ASL)

*American Sign Language (ASL)* is the recognized cultural language of the deaf and hard-of-hearing community. It is a complete and complex language that uses sometimes-intricate hand positions and movement, combined with facial and body expressions, to convey messages. Hearing people use their sense of hearing to communicate with spoken words. Deaf people use their sense of sight to interpret the myriad signs, symbols and gestures used to communicate in sign language.

**The ASL alphabet**

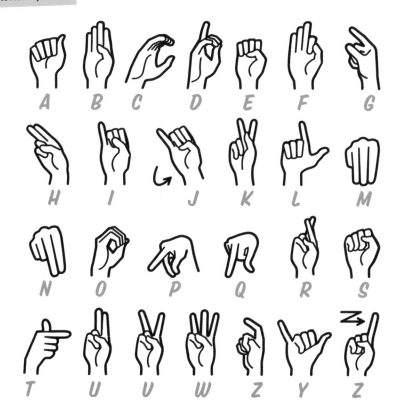

Sign languages have been in use for some 200 years. Like spoken language, sign languages vary from region to region and country to country. Someone who is proficient in ASL may not understand British Sign Language (BSL) and vice versa.

## Intervenor Services for Deafblind People

Deafblind people often make use of an **intervenor** to relay conversations during medical or other appointments or meetings. Intervenor services are exclusively for deafblind individuals. The intervenor works with each individual on a one-to-one basis. They may use a combination of manual sign language and braille to effectively convey spoken communications. There's a cost for this service, and not all provinces or states offer funding.

## FOR THOSE WITH MOBILITY ISSUES

**M**obility aids are devices that help people safely navigate their environments. Blind people use white canes and guide dogs for this purpose. But what options are available to people who do not walk independently?

Walking sticks or canes have been used for centuries to assist with balance and movement. Various styles of crutches are used to provide even greater stability while navigating. Walkers are also in common use today. The concept behind assistive walking aids is that the more points of contact the user has with the ground, the greater the stability. If you can no longer navigate safely on your feet with these aids, the next logical step is to use a wheelchair.

Transport

Manual

Sport

Power

Scooter

The design and performance of wheelchairs have come a long way since 1933, when Harry C. Jennings Sr. and his disabled friend Herbert A. Everest, both mechanical engineers, invented the first lightweight, collapsible, portable steel wheelchair. Today there are five main types of wheelchair: manual, transport, sport, power and scooter.

# EVERY DAY GETS
# BETTER WITH TECHNOLOGY

*don't have to* tell you what a difference the smartphone has made to people's lives. Smartphone technology has had a particularly profound impact on the lives of PWDs—we can now live with ever-increasing independence. Thanks to aggressive advocates for equal access to technology, smartphones are almost completely accessible to most PWDs. I love dictating my texts instead of entering them by hand. Taking notes and pictures and making recordings are a breeze. And then there are the apps. Yes, those amazing apps. Here are a few that have really made a difference to PWDs. They clearly demonstrate the areas in our daily lives where we need assistance.

## For the Blind and Visually Impaired

1. **SEEING AI.** Aim your camera at an object and this app will describe what's in front of it, whether it's a person or an object or a landscape. It can even describe gender and approximate age of a person. Choose a menu or other document, and it will read it to you. It identifies colors. It identifies currency. Take a

pic of a friend, enter the friend's name, then aim the camera at a group, and this app will let you know if your friend is in the crowd. Amazing!

2. **BE MY EYES.** If you'd rather speak to a human for help, this is the app for you. It uses live video chat to connect you to a volunteer set of eyes. Use it while shopping, and the volunteer will describe clothing or food or whatever is in the camera's viewer. Ask the volunteer to tell you the address or name of a store or house and describe the entrance. Lose something in your home? Pan the space and let the volunteer help you find it. I've even used this service to help me assemble a shower caddy. Its only limitation is your imagination.

3. **GPS APPS.** There are many kinds of GPS apps designed to provide blindness-specific information while traveling. Several popular apps are BlindSquare, GetThere and Nearby Explorer.

4. **GROCERY-SHOPPING APPS.** Finding and purchasing grocery items in the store is a nightmare for blind people. Grocery-store apps enable a blind person to view the weekly flyer, browse the aisles and place an order for delivery. These apps are only as good as a store's commitment to creating an accessible shopping experience.

### ARTIFICIAL INTELLIGENCE/REMOTE ASSISTANCE (AIRA)

AIRA is the newest, most innovative service available to blind and visually impaired people. Its assistive service blends wearable technology, artificial intelligence and augmented reality. It uses a network of trained professional agents to remotely assist clients.

Through an app on your smartphone, or through an optional pair of Horizon smart glasses, AIRA delivers access to visual information at the touch of a button. Once connected, an AIRA agent will be at your side to assist you with your tasks. Whether it's shopping for groceries or clothing, exploring unfamiliar places and spaces or simply assisting with tasks that vision loss makes difficult, the AIRA agent is your visual companion. AIRA is a subscription-based service.

## For the Deaf and Hard of Hearing

1. Many television networks and **STREAMING SERVICES** have apps that offer closed-captioning for deaf and hard-of-hearing viewers.

2. **GOOGLE'S LIVETRANSCRIBE** uses automatic speech recognition (ASR) to aid in communication. The phone's microphone picks up the spoken words and simultaneously transcribes them to on-screen text.

3. **AVA** aids in group commu-nication. If a person who is deaf or has hearing loss is with a group of friends, they can get those friends to connect to the app and then see live transcriptions of the group conversation.

4. **CLEAR CAPTIONS**. This app translates all phone calls to text right on screen. If you've ever wondered what it is like to experience hearing loss, check out hearing simulators online. These apps allow you to set them to various hearing levels so a hearing person can experience what someone with hearing loss hears.

## For Wheelchair Users

WheelMate app

1. **FREEWHEEL** is a fitness-tracking app for wheelchair users. It clips to the rim of the wheel of the chair and communicates with your phone's app to deliver all kinds of fitness info.

2. **WHEELMATE** is an essential app that allows users to quickly locate the nearest accessible public washrooms and parking spaces. The app also rates the cleanliness and safety of these spaces.

3. **AXS MAP** identifies and rates businesses in terms of accessibility. It tells the user how many steps there are into the building, whether parking is available, how spacious the interior is in terms of navigating a wheelchair and much more.

4. **UBER** has a strict "equal access for all" policy that guarantees wheelchair users an accessible ride. UberWAV Pilot Program operates in Toronto, Austin, Chicago and London. This project provides accessible transportation to persons who use larger electric wheelchairs and scooters.

Smartphones and personal-assistant devices increase independence in the home as well. Use smart technologies to turn lights on and off, raise and lower window blinds, open and close garage doors and operate the ever-increasing number of smart home appliances.

*Creating prosthetic eyes is a process that combines science and art.*

# LOOKING GOOD WITH PROSTHESES

### Artificial Eyes

Like hearing and walking devices, **prosthetic** eyes, which are created through a blend of science and art, have been around for centuries. After World War II, the United States began to use plastic, a readily available material, to meet the increasing demand for prosthetic eyes by returning war-blinded veterans. Prosthetic eyes were also needed by civilians who had lost an eye or eyes due to disease or trauma. The medical term for the surgical removal of an eye is enucleation.

## IN REAL LIFE

**J**ACQUIE SINCLAIR was born with microphthalmia, a condition in which one or both eyeballs are extremely small. As a baby she underwent surgery to remove one eye and was fitted for a prosthetic eye. Her other eye was removed in her late teens. Jacquie was experiencing chronic pain from an eye disease called glaucoma, and eventually the pain became greater than her fear of losing her only real eye.

After Jacquie's eye was removed, a marble-sized acrylic or silicone implant was inserted into the eye socket. It took three to four weeks for the implant to heal over completely. Jacquie then had her first appointment with an ocularist.

An ocularist fabricates custom prosthetic eyes. The job combines the fields of science and art. There is no actual training program to become an ocularist. Accreditation is achieved after a five-year apprenticeship with a master ocularist.

*Jacquie Sinclair*

The ocularist took an impression of Jacquie's eye socket, using a gel-like substance that hardens quickly. Jacquie says the gel was cool, and the ocularist spread it into every nook and cranny of the socket to create a snug-fitting prosthesis. When the gel dried, the ocularist removed it by tugging on it to break the seal. Jacquie says it was more uncomfortable than painful.

When she returned for her second appointment, she and the ocularist assessed the fit. Then the ocularist determined where the iris should be painted on the surface of the eye shell. At the third appointment, the prosthesis was fitted again, and the iris location was confirmed. The ocularist then added veins to the surface of the prosthesis, ensuring that the colors and patterns were identical to her other prosthetic eye. A light glaze was applied, and once it had dried, the ocularist polished the surface of the eye one last time.

## Artificial Limbs and Other Body Bits

People may lose a limb or limbs in car or workplace accidents, from diseases such as diabetes or after sustaining serious burns.

According to Active Living Alliance Canada, an estimated 227,000 Canadians have an amputation of a limb or extremity from either disease or trauma. Sixty-five percent of lower-limb amputations in Canada are due to complications of diabetes. According to the Amputee Coalition, there are some two million persons with amputations in the United States, where 54 percent of limb loss is caused by vascular disease (diabetes or peripheral arterial disease), 45 percent by trauma and the rest by cancer.

With this amount of limb loss in the United States and Canada, the demand for quality prostheses is increasing. There are four common types of limb prostheses: below-knee, above-knee, below-elbow and above-elbow.

Prosthetic limbs have been in use for some 3,000 years. In the 1500s, the two most-common types were the hand hook and the peg leg.

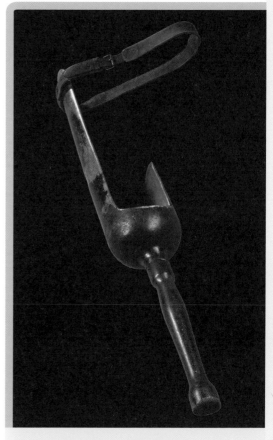

*Prosthetic limbs have come a long way since the days of the wooden peg leg.*

Materials such as metals, wood and fibers were used in the making of the early prostheses. The greatest historical demand for artificial limbs occurred during and after the Civil War in the United States. Today's prostheses are considerably lighter because they are made of plastic, aluminum and composite metals. Each prosthetic device is custom-made to fit the wearer. The cost of a lower-limb prosthesis can range from $5,000 to $50,000. An upper limb costs from $3,000 to $5,000. A prosthesis lasts only three to five years, depending on usage, and coverage of the cost varies greatly from place to place.

So how does one get around the high cost of prostheses? Why not print one off on a 3-D printer? Though not custom-made, such limbs and accessories are fast, affordable alternatives, available to people throughout the world at only a fraction of the cost of traditional prostheses.

The use of microprocessors, computer chips and robotics in the fabrication of prostheses has put the field on an entirely new trajectory. In 2018, engineering students at Johns Hopkins University developed electronic skin (e-dermis.) It fits over the prosthetic hand like a glove and allows the wearer to feel the shape of objects and perceive pain. The next step for the program is to find a way for the e-dermis glove to feel temperature. The ability to detect temperature will alert the wearer to possible problems, thus preventing damage to the expensive prosthesis. Who knows what's next?

Technology continues to offer hope to those experiencing vision loss. The innovative implantable miniature telescope (IMT) is used with patients who have latter-stage age-related macular degeneration.

And in May 2018, researchers at Newcastle University in the United Kingdom 3-D-printed an artificial cornea using a "bio-ink" created by mixing stem cells from a healthy cornea with a gooey material called alginate and a fibrous protein called collagen.

As technologies continue to develop, the options for PWDS may become even more transformative than we can imagine today.

*Dr. Steve Swioklo (left) and Professor Che Connon of Newcastle University watch a 3-D printer make a cornea.*

## —*6*—

# Advocacy and the Politics of Disability

## ADVOCACY IN ACTION

**T**hanks to a lot of the right kind of advocacy, significant progress has been and continues to be made on behalf of PWDs.

Advocating for a better and fuller life is a task most people with disabilities take on at some level. But what if you cannot speak for yourself? What if you're a newborn baby with Down syndrome or another debilitating condition? Who speaks for you then?

Because we live in a time when, for the most part, individual lives are valued, if you are disabled and unable to advocate for yourself, your family and friends can lobby on your behalf for the best possible health care for you. But not that long ago, Alexander Graham Bell, the man we celebrate as the inventor of the telephone, declared his belief in *eugenics*, the controlled selective breeding of human populations.

In a paper presented to the National Academy of Sciences in 1883, Bell said, "Those who believe as I do, that the production of a defective race of human beings would be a great calamity to the world, will examine carefully the causes that lead to the intermarriages of the deaf with the object of applying a remedy."

His belief in eugenics was tied to his conviction that teaching deaf people to speak and lip-read (oralism) was superior because it would ultimately lead to the integration of deaf people into mainstream society. Conversely, he believed that promoting manual speaking (sign language) would lead to the exclusion of deaf people from society and cause them to form their own culture with its own social norms.

## WHAT IS EUGENICS?

Eugenics is the science of "improving" a population by controlled breeding to increase the occurrence of desirable, inheritable characteristics.

## IN REAL LIFE

**A**LBERT RUEL began to lose his vision at the age of 20 because of glaucoma. He chafed at the restrictions that vision loss imposed on him. As he lost more and more of his sight, he noticed more and more limitations on the physical freedoms he'd enjoyed when he had full vision. He no longer felt it was safe to take a brisk walk or go for a run. His world was getting smaller and smaller.

During a family visit to Long Beach, near Tofino on British Columbia's west coast, he rediscovered a freedom he'd thought was lost to him forever.

"A family member asked me if I wanted to go for a run on the beach, and I said no," Albert says. "I was assured the beach was flat and free of debris for as far as the eye could see." He reluctantly agreed to go, and with each stride he began to feel less constrained by his blindness.

Albert Ruel

"I could run free. Each time I heard and felt the slap of the water's edge under my feet, I veered back onto firmer ground." The beach lived up to its name— it stretched on for miles—and there truly were no hazards. This was Albert's first taste of real physical freedom since his diagnosis. He was hooked. He wanted more. And that meant speaking out and getting involved in the politics of disability.

Albert currently works with the Canadian Council of the Blind, a consumer group that manages a national program of assistive-technology clubs for its members and consults on accessibility issues.

## WHAT IS POLITICS?

Politics is a set of activities and beliefs associated with making decisions that apply to people living in groups, such as tribes, cities or countries.

## POLITICS AND THE UNBORN

**T**he influence of politics on the lives of PWDs can start prior to conception. *Genetic testing* may be performed in cases where family histories demonstrate a high-risk factor for such conditions as cystic fibrosis, Down syndrome and disorders specific to various ethnicities, such as sickle cell disease (SCD) and Gaucher disease.

And here's where it gets political. If a fetus tests positive for a certain condition, the parent(s) and medical professionals will discuss risk factors and whether (or not) to continue with the pregnancy. This is a deeply personal decision with life-long implications for everyone involved. How can someone with little or no exposure to the disabled community make such a decision with almost no information or insight?

# THINGS YOU SHOULD KNOW ABOUT PEOPLE WITH DOWN SYNDROME

In a 2013 study reported in the *American Journal of Medical Genetics*, researchers surveyed 284 people 12 years old and older with Down syndrome and asked them questions about their happiness and life satisfaction.

- 99 percent said they were happy with their lives.
- 97 percent liked who they are.
- 96 percent liked how they look.
- 86 percent indicated they could make friends easily.
- Only 4 percent expressed sadness about their life.

The same researchers reported on a second phase of the study in which they interviewed 2,044 parents of children with Down syndrome.

- 99 percent of parents reported that they loved their son or daughter.
- 97 percent were proud of their child.
- 79 percent felt their outlook on life was more positive because of having a child with Down syndrome.
- Only 4 percent regretted having a child with Down syndrome.

*Thalidomide survivor Freddie Astbury was born in 1959 and is the founder of Thalidomide UK.*

# WHEN MEDICAL SOLUTIONS HAVE TRAGIC OUTCOMES

**T**here are times when there can be no foreknowledge of a treatment's side effects. In the late 1950s and early 1960s, a huge pharmaceutical catastrophe resulted in many people in a single generation being born with a disability.

## Thalidomide

In the late 1950s and early '60s, the drug thalidomide was prescribed for pregnant women to ease the discomforts of morning sickness. Unbeknownst to mothers and physicians alike, thalidomide would cause some 10,000 babies to be born with sometimes-devastating birth defects. No data is available on the number of miscarriages that happened because of this drug. Thalidomide affected long-limb development, and babies often were born with short arms and sometimes no recognizable arms at all. Some were born with deformed hands and flippers instead of arms. Many babies had vision damage, along with facial deformities and undeveloped internal organs. The majority of the babies that survived were placed in institutional care because that's how deformed infants were dealt with at that time.

## IN REAL LIFE

**T**RISH JACKSON, born in Australia in 1961, was one of the rare thalidomide babies whose mother loved her just the way she was. Mrs. Jackson refused to place her newborn daughter in institutional care and kept her in the family home. Trish says medical staff would not allow her mother to see her for the first three days of her life because "she was too ghastly to love." Trish lives with constant, severe pain because of her deformed limbs. Fortunately for her, her feet do not cause her pain, and she uses them to do everything—eat with a knife and fork, make detailed sketches and paintings, work in the garden and take photographs. She delivers inspirational anti-bullying presentations to school-age children throughout Australia and is a mother herself.

### Deadly Incubators

In the early 1950s, the incubator was the newest life-saving tool for premature babies. Infants were kept alive in the incubators, receiving warmth and oxygen. Medical staff had no way of knowing the oxygen levels were far too high, and a generation of premature babies was left with damaged retinas, either partially or totally blind.

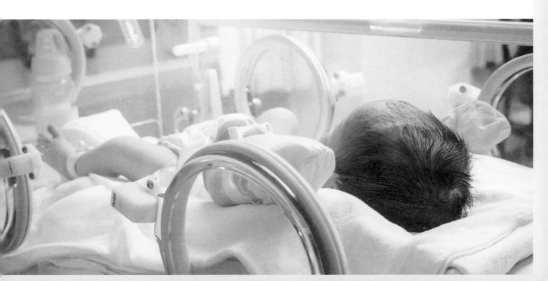

*Gaelynn Lea is a brilliant singer-songwriter and violinist who performs from her wheelchair. She is also a disability-rights activist and the 2016 winner of NPR's Tiny Desk Contest.*

## THE RIGHT TO BE VALUED

**H**istory has taught us that the lives of disabled children and adults have not typically been valued similarly to those of able-bodied children and adults. And what does the present teach us? For years the medical model perceived PWDS as sick or broken, in need of curing and fixing. Thanks to the social model of disability, we now view disability as diversity, because disability is not a disease. When the topic of **medical assistance in dying (MAID)**, or assisted suicide, arises in relation to PWDS, we need to have a clear understanding of what we're looking at.

We don't look at newborn babies and declare them disabled because they cannot walk or talk or care for themselves. Nor do we refer to someone with a chronic, terminal illness as disabled because of their physical and/or mental restrictions. We understand they are in a particular stage of life/being and make decisions accordingly. The disabled body, too, is engaged in the process of living.

The parents of the newborn child are not told their child cannot walk or talk based solely on a single moment in time. Parents will nurture the child, teaching age-appropriate language and mobility skills. Disability isn't unlike the newborn experience.

As new PWDS, we may need to relearn skills like eating, dressing, toileting, etc. A blind person may learn braille and figure out how to navigate with a white cane or guide dog. A deaf person will compensate by learning sign language and/or lipreading. Like the newborn, we learn new skills appropriate to our individual conditions and limitations.

Of course, the waters become muddy when someone is enduring chronic pain and suffering because of a disabling or terminal mental or physical disease. As ethical, moral human beings, do we accept chronic, intolerable pain as an acceptable reason to offer assistance in dying? Problems arise when the decision to end a life is made unilaterally.

On October 24, 1993, Robert Latimer killed his 12-year-old daughter, Tracy, a profoundly disabled child who suffered chronic pain from a severe case of cerebral palsy. Tracy weighed only 40 pounds, and her quadriplegic status meant she was unable to walk, talk or feed herself.

Latimer, a Saskatchewan farmer, freely admitted to not being able to watch the daughter he loved suffer so much. He killed her and spent almost 10 years in prison. He was finally granted day parole in

December 2010. Throughout that time Latimer continued to believe he had given his daughter a merciful death.

Did Latimer's action save his daughter from years of future suffering? Or did it save *him* from years of watching his daughter suffer? PWDS exercise caution in cases like Latimer's, which might inspire other parents to end their child's life for similar reasons.

The main distinction between historical times and the present day is the value society now places on the individual life, able-bodied or disabled. This, coupled with the strict rules and guidelines that are now in place when someone requests assistance in dying in Canada, offers protection for society's most vulnerable citizens. And with this protection, difficult decisions may be made with compassion, creating a positive space for the end of life.

## EUTHANASIA AND ASSISTED DYING: DEFINITIONS OF TERMS

*Euthanasia:* the termination of a patient's life when the patient is suffering from an incurable illness

*Voluntary euthanasia:* ending a life painlessly in accordance with a patient's wishes

*Medical assistance in dying (MAID):* a death that occurs with the assistance of a physician and at the request of the patient

*Assisted dying/assisted suicide:* a suicide in which the act is committed with another person's help
*(From Choosing to Live, Choosing to Die: The Complexities of Assisted Dying by Nikki Tate)*

# THE POLITICS OF EDUCATION AND DISCRIMINATION

*President George H.W. Bush signs the Americans with Disabilities Act of 1990 into law.*

*t's hard to* believe that in the late 1950s and early 1960s, education was not a civil right and was not always readily available to children with disabilities. The thinking was, why would they need an education if they were not expected to live and work in their communities? Fortunately, not everyone thought that way, and members of the disabled-consumer movement and other educational advocates worked hard for the enactment of laws that would ensure the education of disabled children then and in the future. The United Nations Convention on the Rights of Persons with Disabilities, which was adopted in December 2006, is a historic document that came into being with help from strong leadership within the disability community.

## Laws That Protect PWDs in the United States

1.  **THE REHABILITATION ACT OF 1973** "prohibits *discrimination* on the basis of disability in programs conducted by federal agencies, in programs receiving federal financial assistance, in federal employment and in the employment practices of federal contractors."

2. **THE INDIVIDUALS WITH DISABILITIES EDUCATION ACT** is a federal law that requires states and school districts to ensure that children with disabilities receive "a free appropriate public education in the least restrictive environment to their individual needs." This act (under a different name) became law in 1975.

3. **THE AMERICANS WITH DISABILITIES ACT (ADA)**, passed in 1990, is a civil-rights law that prohibits discrimination against individuals with disabilities in all areas of public life, including employment, education, transportation, and public and private places that are open to the general public.

## IN REAL LIFE

**H**ABEN GIRMA is a deafblind California woman who is living proof that access to education works. Deafblind since birth, Girma is a disability-rights attorney and author who balks at the notion that she's an "inspiration." She says, "Some people use it as a disguise for pity. They'll say, 'You're so inspiring,' but in their mind they're thinking, 'Thank God I don't have your problems.'"

A native of Oakland, California, Girma says, "My years of isolation taught me to create the future that I want." Following her 2013 graduation from Harvard Law School, Girma started traveling the world for speaking engagements. "Society is constantly silencing people with disabilities," she says. Girma has a guide dog and communicates via a dual-keyboard system she devised to convert type to braille text. Girma is passionate about internet accessibility, helping to win a landmark case in 2014 against a site that failed to provide access to blind readers. Girma says, "My dream world is a place where people with all types of disabilities are included."

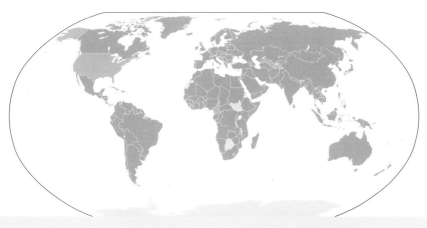

*A map of the world shows the countries that have signed the UN Convention on the Rights of Persons with Disabilities. Parties that have signed and ratified are in purple; parties that have signed but not ratified are in blue. Gray indicates countries that have not signed.*

## Laws That Protect PWDs in Canada

In Canada, the right to an education for able-bodied children is determined by the provinces and territories and their respective education acts. The rights of students with disabilities are contained within provincial *human rights* acts that ensure both access and protection from discrimination for these students. But laws aren't always followed.

In 2012 the Supreme Court of Canada handed down a landmark decision on disability rights. The decision by the highest court in Canada made it law that disabled students are entitled to any supports required during the education process.

Section 15 of the Canadian Charter of Rights and Freedoms makes it clear that every individual in Canada—regardless of race, religion, national or ethnic origin, color, sex, age or physical or mental disability—is to be considered equal. This means that governments must not discriminate on any of these grounds in its laws or programs.

*A disabled veteran's service dog walks on the red carpet in the 2014 America's Parade held on Veterans Day in New York City.*

The Accessible Canada Act was passed into law by the federal government on June 21, 2019. It adds to the existing rights and protections for people with disabilities, which include the Canadian Charter of Rights and Freedoms, the Canadian Human Rights Act and Canada's approval of the United Nations Convention on the Rights of Persons with Disabilities.

Guide Dog Acts and the Service-Animal Acts are laws that permit these specially trained animals to access the same public spaces as their handlers do, such as public transportation, schools, hospitals, restaurants, libraries, recreation centres and any place open to the general public.

In Canada, each province is responsible for drafting its own guide-dog and service-animal act guidelines. Legislation with regard to guide and service animals falls within the jurisdiction of the Americans with Disabilities Act in the United States.

We are most familiar with guide dogs for people with vision loss. These dogs are referred to as guide dogs because that is their primary function. They wear a distinctive harness equipped with a handle that the owner holds on to while moving about.

Service dogs wear vests to identify them as working dogs. They provide emotional and functional support to their owners.

## IN REAL LIFE

**DESPITE LEGISLATION** to ensure that PWDs have equal access to education, equal doesn't necessarily mean optimum. David Lepofsky, a longtime disability-rights advocate who teaches law at University of Toronto and Osgoode Hall, has strong opinions on the subject of equal access to public services such as education.

Lepofsky compares having a disability today as being similar to when women first entered the workforce. There were no washroom facilities for women until they showed up for work, found their voice and spoke up. Lepofsky says, "The world thinks we, the disabled community, is not here or would want to take part."

Lepofsky says that parents simply want to ensure that their kids have an education. He believes that "special education laws are crap," like being given shoes that aren't designed for you and a shoehorn to make them fit.

"You have to fight for years with transit to get someone to tell you what stop you're at," Lepofsky says. He explains that 25 years ago subways and transit buses did not announce the names of stops, so visually impaired travelers couldn't easily know where they were. "We forced them to announce stops, and they finally caught on." The service is helpful not only to visually impaired travelers but also to other transit patrons.

Lepofsky is frustrated with the need to fight the same human-rights battles in every province, saying, "This is the world we face. Instead of having to fight one at a time, we should have inclusive education, transit, health care and other services."

Discrimination against PWDs is a too common experience, despite legislation meant to prevent it. Guide (service) dogs are protected under provincial human-rights legislation. While guide dogs are a common sight in most communities, many service providers lack knowledge of guide-dog legislation.

As a guide-dog user for 14 years, I've been refused entry into restaurants, a doctor's office, a class at a local community college and even a Christmas wreath-making workshop. Yes, I did pass on to Santa the name of the workshop instructor. So, you see, there are laws and then there is justice, the latter being not so easily attained.

Edward Miner Gallaudet

## Deaf Students Speak Out

Bills are tabled and laws are passed, but from time to time they are simply not enough to address a problematic situation. The 1988 political uprising at Gallaudet University in northeast Washington, DC, was one of those situations.

Gallaudet University is the world's only university where all programs and services are specifically designed to accommodate deaf and hard-of-hearing students. It was founded in 1864 when it was granted official university status under the leadership of Edward Miner Gallaudet, its founder and first president, and its charter was signed into law by President Abraham Lincoln that same year. The university also operates an elementary and high school on its grounds. The 2018 enrollment at Gallaudet totaled 1,900 students.

Until 1988 only six individuals had served as president of Gallaudet University in its 124-year history. Six hearing presidents. Yes, hearing presidents, even though Gallaudet University is the world's only postsecondary facility offering university-level programs and services in ASL and written English exclusively for deaf and hard-of-hearing students.

Each president averaged 20 years on the job. In 1987, when the current president resigned, students and alumni decided it was time to have a deaf president for their university. This decision resulted in the first public rebellion by persons with disabilities in North America.

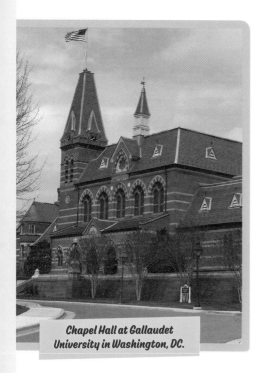

Chapel Hall at Gallaudet University in Washington, DC.

The slogan "Deaf president now!" was the battle cry for alumni and students of Gallaudet. They cited examples from similar educational situations to bolster their demand for a deaf president. Wellesley College, an all-women's institution, has had a female president since its inception, and Yeshiva University, an all-Jewish institution, has had a Jewish president since its inception. Gallaudet supporters were unwilling to settle for anything less than a deaf president.

In March 1988, alumni and students of Gallaudet went on strike to protest the Board of Trustees' appointment of yet another hearing person to the position of president. The board chairperson insisted that deaf people were not able to function in a hearing world. This statement fueled further unrest, because after seven years as chairperson, she had never learned ASL and was unable to speak to the students in their own language.

The students protesting had been born in the early to mid-1960s, when an American rubella (German measles) epidemic doubled the number of deaf students in the education system. It was the era of the civil-rights movement in the United States, and these students expected more for their lives and their futures.

In addition to demanding that a deaf person be brought in as president, students and alumni also demanded there be more deaf board members than hearing ones to better represent the school's student population, and that there be no repercussions for striking students. Since 78 percent of the school's budget came from Congress, the students marched to Congress and found support for their cause from US presidential candidates Bob Dole and George H.W. Bush, who endorsed the students' demands for a deaf president.

One week later both the chair of the board and the newly appointed hearing president resigned after the board met and accepted the students' terms. Gallaudet would finally have its first deaf president.

## THE IMPORTANCE OF PEERS

**P**eer groups offer opportunities for supportive relationships between people with similar lived experiences. Because people are more likely to speak to their peers, these groups promote dialogue, increased self-esteem and confidence, and a shared sense of identity.

PEER GROUPS OFFER
OPPORTUNITIES
FOR SUPPORTIVE
RELATIONSHIPS
BETWEEN PEOPLE
WITH SIMILAR LIVED
EXPERIENCES.

## IN REAL LIFE

**S**HAWN MARSOLAIS knows the value of peer support. She founded Blind Beginnings, a nonprofit agency in Vancouver that's "normalizing blindness for families and kids." Blind Beginnings has been offering recreational, social and blindness-specific skill-development classes exclusively for children since 2008.

Marsolais was diagnosed with a degenerative eye condition at the age of 5 but wasn't told she would eventually lose her sight until she was 12. She didn't want to be different, and she felt broken because her condition was kept a secret.

"I had really low self-esteem going into my teens. I didn't know anyone else who was blind, so I became an overachiever to be seen as equal," she says. She learned to accept her own blindness first and then taught her parents to accept it too.

Marsolais is passionate about working with children and was herself inspired by Daniel Kish, a fellow blind person and motivational speaker who is known for his remarkable navigational abilities. Marsolais says he was so positive, the best role model ever. Their shared love of kids inspired her to start her own program.

Shawn Marsolais

"At present we hold a monthly get-together for the kids where they can get to know one another and work on a project together," Marsolais says. She describes one get-together where each child made a wooden birdhouse from a kit. "It sounds like a regular craft that any kid can do. The added bonus for our kids is that it taught them the concept of a house, that it has a door, walls and a roof just like the houses they live in."

Marsolais is enthusiastic about the future of Blind Beginnings. "The goal is to eventually have a house with a kitchen and stay-in suite for training. We hope to hire our own mobility trainer so we get the services the kids need most. We're also going online to meet increasing service demands from around the province."

## IN REAL LIFE

**T**HANKS TO MACKENZIE (a student at E.C. Drury School for the Deaf) and her best friend, Blair, some Tim Hortons locations are accessible to the hearing-impaired community. Mackenzie and Blair are regulars at the Tim Hortons in Milton, Ontario. "Sometimes it's not so easy to communicate," Mackenzie signs. The girls created and uploaded two videos to YouTube. *Tim Hortons: American Sign Language Vocabulary* is a fun tutorial for staff on how to communicate in ASL using some of Tim Hortons' most iconic words, including *double-double*. *Tim Hortons: Meaningful Gesture* explains that a welcoming Tim Hortons team member makes the difference for Mackenzie and Blair, who together are inspiring change to break down barriers in their community. Their videos were chosen to be part of Tim Hortons' True Stories promotion and are shown on video screens in restaurants across the country. Because of the story, Tim Hortons in Milton has started encouraging staff at their locations to learn some sign language.

## THE POLITICS OF ACCESSIBILITY

**A**ll PWDs need access. The term means something different for each disability. To someone using a wheelchair or with a mobility disability it means physical access—ramps instead of stairs, automatic doors instead of heavy manual doors, lower panels in elevators and, of course, accessible public washrooms.

To a blind person it typically means access to the type of information easily gleaned by someone with sight. One example is printed matter, including books, newspapers, restaurant menus and every type of label or signage you can think of. Another example is access to visual information on television shows and in movies.

A deaf or hard-of-hearing individual faces barriers to audio (sound) information. Unlike blind people, deaf people are able to see their environment. But they are unable to hear spoken words, announcements in public places or sirens while they are driving.

A person with an intellectual challenge has unique access needs, since they struggle with accurately understanding and interpreting their social and physical environments as well as communicating their need for specialized support services.

Limited access to physical spaces and information is, unfortunately, normal for PWDs. Imagine navigating your way through an unfamiliar city with no signage, no streetlights, no information to safely guide you to your destination. The disabled-culture movement strives to fill in these informational and access gaps.

*Daniel Kish is an expert in human echolocation—and an avid cyclist.*

## An Accessibility Tour

Let's take an imaginary tour of a typical older office building and explore its accessibility.

A contractor installing a new ramp in an existing building will often build a ramp over the existing stairs. This usually results in an

incline so steep that someone in a wheelchair could not independently make it up the ramp. It may be a ramp, but in terms of accessibility, it's another barrier. The correct slope ratio is 1:12, which means that every inch of vertical rise requires at least 12 inches of ramp. This creates an incline that most people can navigate.

*This ramp has been constructed in a way that makes it accessible to PWDs.*

*Lower elevator panels with braille below the numbers increase building accessibility for PWDs.*

Okay, you've made it up the ramp. Now let's open the door. Too heavy to open? That's not unusual. Good thing you brought an able-bodied friend to help you. New buildings must now have both exterior and interior push-button, door-opening mechanisms to allow someone with a physical disability to enter.

So now you're in the lobby. Let's check out the elevator. Building codes now require that elevator panels be lowered to a height a wheelchair user can easily reach. This elevator panel conforms to code. Each button on the panel should also be marked in braille. It is, but because the panel is lowered for a wheelchair user, I need to crouch until my hand is level with the braille to be able to read it. However, I doubt there is one design to fit all disabled people. And some braille is definitely better than none.

Now, what about the washroom? The first key characteristic of a truly accessible public washroom is a door that can be opened with one hand because the other hand is needed to negotiate the chair into the room. The second requirement is sufficient space in which to maneuver a wheelchair in and out of a stall, which should have a raised toilet seat and grab bars. So far, so good. But these countertops are too high for the average wheelchair user to comfortably reach the taps, the soap dispenser and/or the paper towels. Reaching for the taps means that clothing may come into contact with the wet countertop. Yes, the sign on the door indicates this washroom is accessible, but there's always room for improvement.

Changes to buildings have come about following years of advocacy about the needs of PWDS. New builds today must conform to the building-code standards that govern the area.

*An accessible bathroom includes all kinds of supports for PWDS.*

# BUILDING CODES

Building-code legislation is required to ensure a consistent housing product. Developers who apply for a building permit are required by law to conform to the standards within the legislation.

Here are some of the considerations that might be included in the part of your local building-code act that covers residential housing and public facilities:

- Corridors, doorways, bathrooms and kitchens that are easier for people with disabilities to use

- Features like easy-to-reach electrical outlets and switches or easy-to-use door and faucet handles

- Building in a way that allows for future installation of items such as grab bars in the bathroom

- Main entrances that include ramps, making it easier for strollers, scootersand wheelchairs to access the building

Here are a few examples that apply specifically to public spaces:

- Increasing accessibility in small retail shops and common areas of condominium and apartment buildings

- Increasing the number of wheelchair spaces required in public viewing spaces

- Equipping courtrooms with assistive listening systems for persons who are deaf or hard of hearing

## Virtual Accessibility

Accessibility also has a virtual aspect. PWDS use the internet each and every day in their busy lives. But there are virtual barriers to access on the internet just as there are barriers in our physical spaces.

Developing accessibility to buildings, buses, planes and trains, and creating access to physical information, is an ongoing process in our changing world. But how exactly is accessibility created when the landscape is digital? What kinds of barriers do PWDS face when they use the internet?

How does someone who is blind access the print and images on-screen? How does someone who is unable to use a mouse because of limited hand movement access the web? How does a deaf person know what information is on a podcast or a video?

# THE WEB ACCESSIBILITY INITIATIVE (WAI)

The World Wide Web Consortium (w3c) was founded in October 1994 by Tim Berners-Lee and is responsible for developing protocols and guidelines that allow the web to continue evolving and growing. One of its initiatives relevant to persons with disabilities was the web accessibility initiative, or WAI.

WAI brings together people from industry, disability organizations, government and research labs around the world to develop guidelines and resources for designing and coding websites to make them accessible to people with auditory, cognitive, neurological, physical, speech and visual disabilities.

*Quadriplegic sailor Hilary Lister on her 26-foot Soling keelboat, Malin. With limited movement of her head only, she used the sip-and-puff method to steer.*

People with visual impairments might use either large-print or screen-reading software to access on-screen information. Large-print software simply enlarges the type for someone who has limited vision to be able to comfortably read it.

Screen-reading software allows a blind person to hear the contents of the screen. Contents are read aloud, and keyboard commands are used to navigate on the page.

How does a developer inform a visually impaired user about an image? The tool used for this is called alternative text for images, or alt text. The developer provides written descriptions of the images within the code, which are read aloud to the visually impaired user.

Someone who cannot use a mouse or a keyboard because of limited hand movement may opt to use a speech-input software program that allows them to give directions verbally. Because this can be a slow process, word-prediction software is usually incorporated. Other technologies, such as sip-and-puff (SNP), allow those with limited manual and speech abilities to access the internet as well.

Sip-and-puff is an assistive technology used to send signals to a device using air pressure. To use a computer, an SNP joystick connected to the mouse input is attached to a breath straw or wand. By inhaling (sipping) or exhaling (puffing) on the straw, the user can manipulate the joystick, which moves the mouse pointer on the screen. Right- or left-clicking and other mouse commands are achieved with specific breath commands.

*Some accessibility barriers are more complicated to avoid, and the solutions take more development time and effort.*

What if someone has limited hand control or a visual impairment and cannot easily or accurately use a mouse? A truly accessible website does not rely exclusively on the use of a mouse. Instead the developer assigns a keystroke or combination of keystrokes to each and every mouse function.

Keyboard commands, or hot keys, are available through the Help menu in software applications that follow WAI standards. Yes, it requires a lot of memorization, but it can be done.

Just as images aren't available to people who can't see, audio files aren't available to people who can't hear. Providing a text transcript makes the audio information accessible to people who are deaf or hard of hearing, as well as to search engines and other technologies that can't hear. Some accessibility barriers are more complicated to avoid, and the solutions take more development time and effort. WAI provides developers with extensive resources to help, such as tutorials and support materials. It has developed similar standards and tools for the development of smartphone apps.

*Sometimes an individual decides to challenge the system and sets a positive precedent for the future.*

## DISABILITY RIGHTS ARE HUMAN RIGHTS

**T**he *disability-rights movement* focuses on issues of chronic poverty, unemployment, educational exclusion and discriminatory housing practices faced by PWDs. Numerous individuals and consumer-advocacy organizations work together to lobby local, provincial and state, and federal governments to pass legislation to protect PWDs in these areas. Sometimes an individual decides to challenge the system and sets a positive precedent for the future. Justin Clark (see sidebar) is one of those individuals.

## IN REAL LIFE

**J**USTIN CLARK was born with cerebral palsy. On the advice of medical staff, his parents placed him in an institution outside of Ottawa, Ontario, in 1964, when he was two. He was one of 2,000 residents housed in this facility. His parents, who were also his legal guardians, did not believe Justin would ever have the capacity to make good, informed decisions about his care and living situation. Almost 20 years later, Justin fought back by suing his own parents.

In a landmark court decision in 1982, Justin won his case by proving that he did indeed have the mental capacity to make his own decisions about how and where he lived and that he no longer required legal guardianship.

He forever changed the Canadian legal landscape by paving the way for people with disabilities to have a greater say in how and where they live their lives.

At the time of this writing, Justin is in his mid-50s. He maintains a close relationship with his parents and siblings, despite the court case. He has traveled extensively throughout the world, works in the technology field and continues to live the independent lifestyle he worked so hard to attain.

## DISABILITY AND THE LAW

**P**eople with disabilities are vulnerable to discrimination of many types. Being refused a job on the grounds of disability or being denied housing by a landlord or strata council are not uncommon examples of discrimination PWDS face on a regular basis. If they decide to pursue legal remedies, they have to engage with the justice system, which can be complex and frustrating on several levels.

The average person seldom comes into close contact with the legal system so has limited knowledge of how to navigate the process. When you eventually find the information you need, it's time to start the paperwork. Paperwork is a barrier to most PWDs. To a blind person, it means having to enlist the services of a friend to help. Someone with physical challenges may not have the manual dexterity to fill out the documentation. And to someone with an intellectual impairment, the process is simply too lengthy and confusing to tackle.

*Paperwork is a barrier to most PWDs. To a blind person, it means having to enlist the services of a friend to help.*

In order to proceed further, you may need to hire a lawyer. If you can't afford one, you may have to contact a local law-student legal clinic at no cost to you. While such clinics are helpful to many people, your time with a student lawyer is brief at best.

## No Guide Dogs Allowed

I used the services of a law-student legal clinic when I decided to lodge a human-rights complaint against a local doctor who refused to treat me if I brought my dog along with me into the exam room. He believed my dog posed an allergy threat to other patients. I was the only patient in the waiting room, and I could tell that the chair I was sitting in was upholstered and the floor beneath my feet was carpeted, hardly choices indicative of someone concerned about allergies. While I waited for the doctor, an acquaintance of mine entered the office. She offered to sit with my dog in the waiting room while I went in to see the doctor. When I entered the examination room, it too had an upholstered chair and carpeting on the floor. Little did the doctor know, but my dog and I had just gotten off a transit bus filled to capacity with the after-work crowd, and no one had suffered any ill effects because of my dog. I too have allergies. My dog is a standard poodle, a breed that is almost 100 percent hypoallergenic.

The young law student I worked with seemed uncomfortable in my presence. She stuttered and stammered in an effort not to say the wrong thing to someone with a disability. She seemed overwhelmed with trying to comprehend the spectrum of visual impairment, how a guide dog does its job and how I managed with such little vision. My complaint was dismissed. I believe a more mature, experienced lawyer would have achieved more positive results. But a lawyer charges approximately $350 an hour. The laws are in place and low-cost legal services are available, but sometimes you get what you pay for.

Jacquie Sinclair has experienced numerous refusals to accommodate her guide dog too. She was refused a medical consultation at a local walk-in clinic because of her guide dog. She explained the law to the doctor, but he responded by saying that he was allergic to dogs and had his rights too. She didn't know her way to any other clinics, so she went home. She saw her GP the next day and was diagnosed with full-on pneumonia. Where do human rights begin and end? Does one right trump another right? Whatever happened to compassion and compromise?

Parents or family members may come into contact with the political world of disability when they advocate for fair treatment of a family member by an educational or medical institution or even an employer.

In Canada, each province has its own human-rights code that sets out the laws for the province. Tribunals hear the complaints and make their decisions based on the facts as presented by the complainant and the defendant. Provincial human-rights tribunals handle cases such as discrimination by employers, housing providers and service providers.

Because the United States has the Americans with Disabilities Act in place nationally, complaints alleging disability discrimination by a state or local government or a public accommodation (private business) may be filed with the US Department of Justice's Civil Rights Division, Disability Rights Section, in Washington, DC. Complaints are reviewed and then forwarded to relevant agencies for possible mediation and/or litigation.

# THE POLITICS OF DISABILITY IN SPORTS

**T**he individuals and organizations who speak out for improved services for people with disabilities represent a grassroots, consumer-driven political movement. Political movements don't always use a collective voice to convey their message. Sometimes they let their bodies do the talking.

## IN REAL LIFE

**A**T AGE 21, LEE DUCKHEE was the first deaf player in the Association of Tennis Professionals (ATP). Duckhee has been playing the game since he was seven, but he doesn't want to be defined by his deafness, which was first diagnosed when he was a toddler. Duckhee compensates for his hearing loss with his keen vision, focusing on his opponent's swing, contact with the ball, and the speed and spin of the ball as it hurtles toward him. He watches not only the game but also the umpire's hand gestures to follow the scoring.

Lee Duckhee

Duckhee wants other PWDs to know that hard work will allow them to achieve their goals.

# PLAYING THE GAMES

## The Paralympic Games

British neurologist Sir Ludwig Guttmann had a game-changing passion for using sports in the rehabilitation of people with spinal-cord injuries. He presented a competition involving 16 of his patients at the opening ceremonies of the 1948 Olympic Games in London. By 1952 he had introduced the world to the games that would later be called the Paralympic Games.

Guttmann is quoted as saying, "If I ever did one good thing in my medical career it was to introduce sport into the rehabilitation of disabled people." Prior to Guttmann's revolutionary sports-as-therapy approach, patients with spinal-cord injuries were kept in hospital and

*Australian Paralympian Eric Russell shakes hands with Sir Ludwig Guttmann, founder of the Paralympic Games, at the 1976 Summer Paralympics.*

made comfortable for the duration of their lives, which often was as short as two years. Efforts to include more and more people with disabilities continued for the following decades.

The first official Paralympic Winter Games were held in Sweden in 1976. Since that time summer and winter Paralympic Games have been held every four years, immediately following the Olympic Games.

Jessica Frotten

**F YOU THINK THIS CRASH LOOKS BAD,** you're right. It happened at the 2018 Commonwealth Games on Australia's Gold Coast. Jessica Frotten, a 29-year-old wheelchair racer from Canada, was competing in the 1,500-meter race when the crash took place.

"I'll never forget it," Jessica says. "That race molded me." She was mad, sad and embarrassed. "I put everything into that race. But that's the way sports is. It made me a stronger racer."

Jessica has known far worse than that collision. At age 21 she was in a car crash on the Alaska Highway, sustaining a torn aorta, a broken clavicle, a punctured lung, two broken feet, broken ribs and a severed spine at the T10 vertebra. Her injuries left her with paraplegia.

Following a three-month stay in the ICU in Edmonton, Alberta, Jessica started on the next phase of healing—rehabilitation. She says she tried wheelchair basketball and rugby but didn't feel the passion. When she tried racing, though, she knew she'd found her sport. "I fell in love with it the very first time."

Jessica's story is another example of how sport can play an important role in the lives of PWDs. "My life started when I started racing," says Jessica. It provided her with the feeling she was once again moving forward in her life.

In addition to her busy training schedule, she works full-time as a transition specialist with the local rehabilitation center in Regina, Saskatchewan. She says she loves her work, getting to meet newly injured people and recommending specialty products to assist in their therapy. She mentors both children and adults in her work, quietly showing them how one day they too can have a full and rewarding life.

*The German basketball team battles Spain during the 2019 Special Olympics World Games at the Abu Dhabi National Exhibition Centre.*

## The Special Olympics

Like so many monumental innovations, the Special Olympics was inspired by someone with a disabled family member. Eunice Kennedy Shriver was the fifth of nine children of Joseph P. and Rose Fitzgerald Kennedy. Her older sister, Rosemary, had an intellectual impairment. Shriver noticed that most people with intellectual disabilities were excluded and routinely placed in *custodial institutions*. They were often ignored and neglected, yet she knew they had many talents and gifts to offer. An athlete herself, Eunice believed that sports could be a common ground to unite people with intellectual impairments from around the world.

*Eunice Kennedy Shriver*

In summer of 1962, Shriver hosted a sports day in her backyard for her sister and other intellectually impaired children, an annual event that came to be known as Camp Shriver. What began as Shriver's vision evolved into Special Olympics International—a global movement that today serves more than 4.7 million people with intellectual disabilities in 170 countries.

## The Invictus Games

The Invictus Games is an international, adaptive-sport competition for wounded service men and women, as well as veterans, founded by Harry, Duke of Sussex in 2013. It is yet another example of a political movement that empowers its membership through excellence in sport. *Invictus* means "unconquered," and the motto of the games is I Am Unconquered.

*Harry, Duke of Sussex, founder of the Invictus Games, meets a competitor in Toronto in 2017.*

The first competition was held in 2014 in London, followed by games in Florida in 2016, Toronto in 2017 and Sydney, Australia, in 2018. The Sydney games hosted over 500 competitors from 19 nations, who participated in 10 adaptive sports, including archery, cycling, power lifting and wheelchair basketball. Sports provide many PWDs with a freedom of movement they feared they would never feel again, as well as fitness, goals and a sense of achievement, elements we all need in our lives to be happy, productive citizens.

# DISABILITY IN POPULAR CULTURE

*Ryan O'Connell*

**A**lso referred to as the "culture of the people," popular culture (or pop culture) is transmitted through mass media and serves to unite people through music, movies, television and leisure activities. As accessible technologies improve, more and more opportunities exist for inclusion of PWDs in popular culture.

"I think that disability representation is, like, the last to the representation party. Like, maybe that party wasn't accessible," says Ryan O'Connell, the creator behind the Netflix series *Special*. Based on his own life, the series is about a millennial gay man with cerebral palsy who is trying to make it as a writer. O'Connell and his cast have earned four Emmy nominations for the show.

In June 2019, Broadway star Ali Stroker became the first person in a wheelchair to win a Tony Award for her performance in *Oklahoma!*

## Disability on Reality TV

Reality TV gets a thumbs-up for its inclusion of PWDS in its programming. Disabled comedian Ryan Niemiller finished third in season 14 of *America's Got Talent* in 2019. Ryan was born with foreshortened arms and missing fingers on both hands. His routine addresses disability with stories of dating, finding a job and much more. Ryan was the second PWD to appear

*Nyle DiMarco*

on the show. Blind musician and singer Kodi Lee wowed audiences that same season, finishing in first place. *Dancing with the Stars* gets five stars for its inclusion of PWDS on its long-running series. Its 2016 winner, Nyle DiMarco, who is totally deaf, was the second deaf contestant on the show.

Legally blind singer Shayla Winn earned a trip to Hollywood in 2019 with her impressive performance on *American Idol*.

*RJ Mitte, Zack Gottsagen and Danny Woodburn at the 2019 ReelAbilities Film Festival opening night and gala in Universal City, CA.*

## Disability Film Festivals

Like Netflix star Ryan O'Connell, hundreds of filmmakers with disabilities have access to two major film festivals run exclusively by PWDS for PWDS, and, yes, the events are accessible.

ReelAbilities Film Festival is the largest festival in the United States dedicated to promoting awareness and appreciation of the lives, stories and artistic expression of people with different disabilities. Founded in 2007, the festival presents award-winning films by and about people with disabilities. ReelAbilities events are now held in more than 20 cities, including in Canada.

Superfest International Disability Film Festival is the longest-running disability film festival in the world. Since it first debuted in 1970, Superfest has celebrated cutting-edge cinema that portrays disability through a diverse, complex, unabashed and engaging lens.

## INCLUSIVE TOYS

Even the toy industry is stepping up to the inclusion plate thanks to organizations like #ToyLikeMe, a UK-based advocacy group promoting toys that reflect kids with disabilities.

#ToyLikeMe takes mainstream toys, adapts them to reflect the children with disabilities who play with them, and has successfully put pressure on some toy companies to incorporate those changes in one or more of their toys.

Renée Fabian, news and lifestyle editor for *The Mighty*, says, "Children need toys that reflect themselves and the diversity of the world around them. Toys teach children from a very young age what 'normal' is."

## Disability in Social Media

PWDS are making inclusion inroads in social media too. No matter the disability and associated issues, there's a blog or website about it. With the web's commitment to accessibility, social-media apps and opportunities are available to everyone. Snapchat, Instagram and Facebook are all accessible platforms.

## IN REAL LIFE

**MOLLY BURKE** is a 27-year-old visually impaired woman from Oakville, Ontario, who has embraced social media in her commitment to get the anti-bullying message out. Burke's popularity and her disability messaging have garnered a social-media following of nearly two million YouTube subscribers. Burke started experiencing a gradual loss of vision as a young child and had lost all sight by the time she was 14. She talks candidly about her experiences as a teen and young woman with a disability, ranting

*Molly Burke with Gallop*

when she's frustrated because of her disability and enthusiastic when she gives her online fashion and makeup tutorials. Burke's message of hope is also captured in her 2019 *New York Times* bestselling memoir entitled *It's Not What It Looks Like*.

## RELAXED PERFORMANCES

Not only are PWDs enjoying more access in their lives, but their quad-ruped companions are too. A group of service dogs in training, ranging from poodles to golden retrievers, took in a production of *Billy Elliot the Musical* at the Stratford Festival in Canada. The dogs were learning to sit quietly in the theater during a ***relaxed performance***, which is designed for people with autism and those who find theater noises too startling. Like closed-captioning for deaf people and described audio for blind theater-goers, relaxed performances are another way of ensuring inclusion in the world of live theater.

## WHAT CAN YOU DO?

**N**ow *that you've* read this book and understand the world of otherness a bit better, the question remains: What can one nondisabled person do?

1. **GET TO KNOW US.** Why not volunteer? If you like cycling or other sports and/or recreational activities, PWDs could really use your assistance. If you like sorting through lots and lots of paper, I could use a hand too.

2. **PURSUE ACADEMIC OPPORTUNITIES IN DISABILITY RESEARCH.** Policymakers need current academic research on disability issues so they can create policies with the disabled community in mind.

3. **IF YOU'RE A SCIENCE AND ENGINEERING ENTHUSIAST,** the disabled community needs you! Technology is playing such an important role for us and will continue to do so. We need smart engineers to develop safe self-driving car technology. Robotics are the key to increased function for a lot of us. We need fine-arts people too. Who do you think make prosthetic eyes and the prosthetic skin on artificial limbs look so real?

4. **AND IF YOU DO NOTHING ELSE, PLEASE, PLEASE VOTE** as soon as you are allowed to. Find out about your local politicians—city, province or state, and federal. Call their offices and ask them where they stand regarding affordable housing and health-care services for PWDs. Would they support an increase in the amount of disability pension to bring recipients above the poverty line? If you don't agree with their policies, you don't have to vote for them. You get to speak with your vote. It's important.

# A FINAL WORD FROM THE AUTHOR

**M**y goal in writing this book has been to demystify the world of disability and otherness enough that you will now view PWDS with a discerning eye. You'll be able to distinguish individual types of disabilities rather than lumping them together. You'll understand that our independence may look different than yours and that our presence and inclusion are here to stay. The more we PWDS learn and share, the more we benefit.

When people comment that I don't look "all that blind" and that I do so well, I tell them I'm good at being blind because I am. I subscribe to journalist Malcolm Gladwell's 10,000-Hour Rule. Gladwell says that if you practice something—a craft, an art, a skill—for 10,000 hours, you can't help but be good at it. By that measure, I'm an expert! Living with a disability is a personal process of discovery. I know because I'm living the process.

My research experience for this topic was lengthy, inspiring and sometimes shocking. The chapter on the history of disability was particularly difficult. Stories of abandoned disabled infants, the use of PWDS as entertainment and the wholesale institutionalization of generations of PWDS was beyond disheartening. You might say the treatment of PWDS throughout history was "how it was back then." I get that. It's not like that now. I get that too. But why does the historical record show centuries of abuse toward its marginalized citizens? Are societies hardwired to reject the *other*?

The good news is that you and your peers, as well as young PWDS, are a generation capable of great learning and positive change. If you put down this book and think, "Hey, we're pretty much all the same—we can do this," then I'd say I've done my job.

# Acknowledgments

Special thanks to Lynne Van Luven for her ongoing support and friendship.

Thanks also to Sarah Harvey, editor and word polisher extraordinaire, and the staff of Orca Book Publishers for making all our hard work look great.

Many thanks also to those of you who shared your stories: Albert Ruel, Wendy Cox, Shawn Marsolais, Jacquie Sinclair, Gail Bishop, Heather Bergink and Jessica Frotten. Thanks also to Elizabeth Metcalfe and Pat Danforth for their perusal of the manuscript for accuracy.

# Glossary

**accessibility**—the design of products, devices, services or environments for people with disabilities; the "ability to access" and benefit from some system or entity

**acquired disability**—a disability whose onset occurs after birth

**activities of daily living (ADL)**—key daily tasks, such as the ability to eat, bathe and dress independently, which are assessed to determine level of physical disability

**adaptive behavior**—an individual's ability to apply social and practical skills in everyday life

**adaptive clothing**—clothing that takes into account the limited ranges of motion some disabled people experience

**adaptive technology**—special versions of already existing technologies or tools that provide enhancements or different ways for PWDs to interact with technology

**American Sign Language (ASL)**—the recognized cultural language of the deaf and hard-of-hearing community in North America

**braille**—a form of written language for blind people in which characters are represented by patterns of raised dots that are read with the fingertips

**carded athlete**—an elite disabled athlete who receives government funding to assist with living and training expenses

**closed-captioning**—
text subtitles for the deaf
or hard of hearing

**cochlear implant**—a small,
complex electronic device
that can help provide a sense
of sound to a person who is
profoundly deaf or severely
hard of hearing

**cognitive ability, or
intellectual functioning**—
ability to plan, comprehend
and reason

**congenital disability**—
a disability present at birth

**cultural norms**—
the shared expectations and
rules that guide the behavior
of people within social groups

**culture of disability**—
societal awareness that
empowers PWDS and gives
them a collective voice

**custodial institutions**—
establishments mandated to
take over the housing and care
of an individual, such as prisons,
detention centers, psychiatric
hospitals and residential schools

**custom-transit service**—
a company with a fleet of
wheelchair-accessible vehicles
that provides door-to-door
service for disabled individuals unable to use the regular
transit system

**deafblindness**—a condition
in which there is substantial
loss of both vision and hearing,
making it difficult to communicate, socialize, navigate and
access information

**disability**—a physical or mental
condition that limits a person's
movements, senses or activities

**disability studies**—an
academic discipline that examines the meaning, nature
and consequences of disability

**discrimination**—the unjust or prejudicial treatment of groups of people or things, especially on the grounds of race, age, disability or sex

**euthanasia**—the termination of a person's life when they are suffering from an incurable illness

**genetic testing**—medical testing that identifies changes in chromosomes, genes or proteins

**group home**—a private house with multiple rental rooms available to PWDs, often funded and run by nonprofit housing societies

**haptic**—relating to or based on the sense of touch

**human rights**—rights inherent to all human beings, regardless of race, sex, nationality, ethnicity, language, religion or any other factor

**incentive program**—an employment program that gives PWDs a chance to prove they can be a real asset in the workplace while minimizing the financial risk to the employer

**inclusive**—welcoming to all kinds of people

**integration**—the action or process of successfully joining or mixing with a different group of people

**intellectual disability**—limitations in cognitive ability or intellectual functioning, and in adaptive behavior

**intervenor**—someone who works exclusively with deafblind individuals on a one-to-one basis to convey spoken communications

**invisible disability**—a disability we cannot see, such as deafness, a learning disorder or intellectual impairment

**legal blindness**—a level of blindness that has been defined by law to limit some activities (such as driving) for safety reasons or to determine eligibility for disability-related government programs and benefits

**legal deafness**—a level of deafness that has been defined by law to limit some activities for safety reasons or to determine eligibility for disability-related government programs and benefits

**LGBTQ+**—abbreviation for lesbian, gay, bisexual, transgender and queer

**mainstreaming**—integrating students with disabilities into general-education classrooms

**marginalized**—placed in a position of marginal importance, influence or power

**medical assistance in dying (MAID)**—death that occurs with the assistance of a physician and at the request of the patient

**mobility**—the ability to move or be moved freely and easily

**mobility aids**—devices designed to assist in walking or other kinds of movement for people with a mobility impairment

**nonprofit housing**—housing for those who wish to live independently but still require subsidized rent and care assistance

**paraplegia**—paralysis of the legs and lower body, typically caused by spinal injury or disease

**prosthetic**—of or relating to a prosthesis, an artificial device that replaces or augments a missing or impaired body part

**PWD(S)**—person(s) with a disability or disabilities

**quadriplegia**—paralysis of all four limbs, typically caused by spinal injury or disease

**relaxed performance**—a type of theater performance that addresses the low-stimulation requirements of persons with autism

**segregation**—the action or state of setting someone or something apart from other people or things

**sensory disability**—a severe impairment of or loss of the sense of sight and/or hearing

**social housing**—subsidized developments owned and managed by the state, by nonprofit organizations or by a combination of the two, with the aim of being affordable

**visible disability**—a disability that is easily recognizable

**warehousing**—the practice of placing people, typically prisoners, the disabled or psychiatric patients, in large, impersonal institutions

# Resources

## CANADA

Active Living Alliance for Canadians with a Disability: *ala.ca*
Autism Society Canada: *autismcanada.org*
Canadian Association of the Deaf: *cad.ca*
Canadian National Institute for the Blind: *cnib.ca*
Council of Canadians with Disabilities: *ccdonline.ca*
DisAbled Women's Network Canada: *dawncanada.net*
International Paralympic Committee: *paralympic.org/canada*
Rick Hansen Foundation: *rickhansen.com*

## UNITED STATES

American Association of Adapted Sports Programs: *adaptedsports.org*
American Association of People with Disabilities: *aapd.com*
American Council of the Blind: *acb.org*
Amputee Coalition of America: *amputee-coalition.org*
Autism Society: *autism-society.org*
Hearing Loss Association of America: *hearingloss.org*
Helen Keller National Center for Deaf-Blind Youths & Adults: *helenkeller.org*
National Federation of the Blind: *nfb.org*
United Spinal Association: *unitedspinal.org*

## INTERNATIONAL RESOURCES

Amputee Coalition: *amputee-coalition.org*

Autism Network International: *autismnetworkinternational.org*

Disability Rights International: *driadvocacy.org*

Disabled Peoples' International: *dpi.org*

Global Down Syndrome Foundation: *globaldownsyndrome.org*

International Disability Alliance: *internationaldisabilityalliance.org*

International Paralympic Committee: *paralympic.org*

International Spinal Cord Society: *iscos.org.uk*

Invictus Games: *invictusgamesfoundation.org*

Special Olympics: *specialolympics.org*

World Blind Union: *worldblindunion.org*

World Federation of the Deaf: *wfdeaf.org*

Links to external resources are for personal and/or educational use only and are provided in good faith without any express or implied warranty. There is no guarantee given as to the accuracy or currency of any individual item. The author and publisher provide links as a service to readers. This does not imply any endorsement by the author or publisher of any of the content accessed through these links.

For a complete list of references, visit the page for this book on our website (orcabook.com).

# Photo Credits

## CHAPTER FOUR

p. 62: Hannalora Leavitt; p. 63: AnnaStills/Shutterstock.com; p. 65: photofort77/Shutterstock.com; p. 66: WAYHOME studio/Shutterstock.com; p. 68: xavieramau/Getty Images; p. 71: Kathy Hutchins/ Shutterstock.com; p. 72: Bahereh Hosseini/Barcroft Images/Getty Images; p. 76: Tony Giles; p. 77: Hannalora Leavitt; p. 78: courtesy of Amar Latif, Founder of Traveleyes; p. 80: FXQuadro/ Shutterstock.com; courtesy of Banman Photography for Blind Golf Canada; p. 82: ID1974/Shutterstock.com; p. 83: MikeDotta/Shutterstock.com; p. 84: Marco Ciccolella/Shutterstock.com; p. 86: RacheeLynn/ Shutterstock.com; p. 87: ACHPF/Shutterstock.com; p. 88: Travability Images/Shutterstock.com; p. 91: LWA/Dann Tardif/Getty Images; p. 92: fizkes/Getty Images; p. 97: Ivanka Kunianska/Shutterstock.com

## CHAPTER FIVE

p. 100: Andrey_Popov/Shutterstock.com; p. 101: Kritzolina/Wikimedia Commons (CC BY-SA 4.0); 102: George Grantham Bain Collection [Public domain]/Wikimedia Commons; p. 103: Hannalora Leavitt; p. 104: Satellite Photos/Shutterstock.com; p. 105: SNP_SS/Shutterstock.com; p. 106: Snowman 2016/ Shutterstock.com; p. 107: Movierain/Wikimedia Commons (CC BY-SA 3.0); p. 108: Nadezda Murmakova/ Shutterstock.com; p. 109: Science Museum, London/Wellcome Collection (CC BY 4.0); p. 110: Monika Wisniewska/Shutterstock.com; p. 112: RRA79/Shutterstock.com; p. 113 (top to bottom): GeniusKp/ Shutterstock.com, xiaorui/Shutterstock.com, daseaford/Shutterstock.com, daseaford/Shutterstock.com, CharlotteRaboff/Shutterstock.com; p. 115: Halfpoint/Shutterstock.com; p. 117: Ava.me (www.ava.me); p. 118: Coloplast Canada; p. 119: Terelyuk/Shutterstock.com; p. 120: Jacquie Sinclair; p. 121: Science Museum, London/Wellcome Collection (CC BY 4.0); p. 122: DGLImages/Shutterstock.com; p. 123: John Millard Photography

## CHAPTER SIX

p. 127: Albert Ruel; p. 130: Paul Cooper/Shutterstock.com; p. 131: Kwangmoozaa/Shutterstock.com; p. 132: Paul Vienneau (see also violinscratches.com); p. 135: Unknown author [Public domain]/Wikimedia Commons; p. 137: adapted from L.tak [Public domain]/Wikimedia Commons; p. 138: Glynnis Jones/ Shutterstock.com; p. 140: Mathew Brady [Public domain]/Wikimedia Commons; p. 142: Andrew Kuchling from Vienna, Virginia, USA/Wikimedia Commons (CC BY-SA 2.0); p. 144: Richard Bailey/Getty Images; p. 145: Shawn Marsolais; p. 147: PopTech/Wikimedia Commons (CC BY-SA 2.0); p. 148 (top): Ethan Boisvert/ Shutterstock.com; p. 148 (bottom): SolStock/Getty Images; p. 149: chanida pp/Shutterstock.com; p. 150: wk1003mike/Shutterstock.com; p. 151: Anderson Ross Photography Inc/Getty Images; p. 153: Mark Lloyd/Shutterstock.com; p. 160: Bryan Pollard/Shutterstock.com; Australian Paralympic Committee/Wikimedia Commons (CC BY-SA 3.0); p. 162: Dean Lewins/EPA-EFE/Shutterstock.com; p. 163 (top): dominika zara/Shutterstock.com; p. 163 (bottom): Bill Golladay/Wikimedia Commons (CC BY-SA 4.0); p. 164: ACHPF/Shutterstock.com; p. 165: Michael Mattes/Shutterstock.com; p. 166 (top): Kathy Hutchins/Shutterstock.com; p. 166 (bottom): Tommaso Boddi/Getty Images; p. 167: toylikeme.org; p. 168: Kathy Hutchins/Shutterstock.com; p. 169: K-9 Country Inn Service Dogs

## ACKNOWLEDGMENTS

p. 172: Denis Kuvaev/Shutterstock.com

*Every effort has been made to locate and credit the correct copyright owners of the images used in this book. The publisher apologizes for any errors or omissions and would be grateful if notified of corrections that should be made in future reprints or editions.*

# Index

# CONTINUE THE CONVERSATION

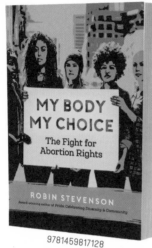